STUDENTS AT THE CENTER

FEMINIST ASSESSMENT

Edited by Caryn McTighe Musil

ASSOCIATION OF AMERICAN COLLEGES AND
NATIONAL WOMEN'S STUDIES ASSOCIATION, 1992

THIS WORK WAS SUPPORTED BY
THE FUND FOR THE IMPROVEMENT
OF POSTSECONDARY EDUCATION,
U.S. DEPARTMENT OF EDUCATION

GENERAL EDITOR: CARYN McTIGHE MUSIL

COVER: Quilt from the collection of
Marjorie A. Laidman (detail).
Courtesy of
Hearts and Hands Media Arts
San Francisco, California
(415) 550-2353

Published by
Association of American Colleges
1818 R Street, NW
Washington, D.C. 20009

Copyright 1992

ISBN 0-911696-56-3
Library of Congress Catalog No. 92-71981

CONTENTS

PROJECT PARTICIPANTS
1992

Project Director
CARYN McTIGHE MUSIL
Senior Research Associate
Association of American Colleges

Project Associate
SUZANNE HYERS
Meeting Coordinator
Association of American Colleges

National Assessment Team
CAROLYNE W. ARNOLD, University of Massachusetts–Boston
LEE KNEFELKAMP, Teachers College, Columbia University
JILL MATTUCK TARULE, University of Vermont
JOAN POLINER SHAPIRO, Temple University
MARY KAY THOMPSON TETREAULT,
California State University–Fullerton

External Evaluator
PAT HUTCHINGS, American Association for Higher Education

Project Coordinators, Participating Colleges and Universities
ANITA CLAIR FELLMAN, Old Dominion University
LAURIE A. FINKE, Lewis and Clark College
ROSANNA HERTZ, Wellesley College
MARY JO NEITZ, University of Missouri–Columbia
MICHELE PALUDI, City University of New York–Hunter College
SUSAN REVERBY, Wellesley College
LINDA R. SILVER, Oberlin College
JOAN TRONTO, City University of New York–Hunter College
GAY VICTORIA, University of Colorado
JEAN WARD, Lewis and Clark College
MARCIA WESTKOTT, University of Colorado
BARBARA A. WINSTEAD, Old Dominion University

ACKNOWLEDGMENTS

Students at the Center: Feminist Assessment is the last of the publications to emerge from a three-year research project on women's studies and student learning funded by the U.S. Department of Education's Fund for the Improvement of Postsecondary Education (FIPSE). During this last year, both FIPSE's Program Officer, Helene Scher, and its Deputy Director, Thomas C. Carroll, provided invaluable administrative support for the project. I am indebted to them for their counsel and their intervention.

As with the June publication of *The Courage to Question: Women's Studies and Student Learning*, the Association of American Colleges (AAC) has functioned this past year and a half as the administrative home for the project, providing office space, financial support, and the companionship of congenial colleagues. It has been a fruitful collaboration between AAC and the National Women's Studies Association (NWSA), where the grant originated. I am especially indebted to Paula P. Brownlee, president of AAC, and to AAC's executive vice president, Carol G. Schneider, both of whom have been unflagging in their belief in the importance of the project and in the insights women's studies can contribute to larger questions facing higher education today.

As with the previous project publications, we have profited from the expertise of the Office of Public Information and Publications at AAC. Once more, we have benefitted from the skills of Kristen A. Lippert-Martin, who is no longer with AAC but was willing to edit this final publication. Acting Director of Public Information and Publications David M. Stearman, with his usual sharp wit and keen eye, oversaw the production process with support from Holly Madsen, assistant editor, and Cynthia Brooker, production editor.

Loretta Younger, office manager at NWSA, helped with some of the administrative financial details, doing so with her characteristic cheerfulness.

Although she had begun a demanding new job as meeting coordinator at AAC before *Students at the Center* was completed, Suzanne Hyers, former project associate with the grant, continued to provide administrative and editorial support for this last volume and also authored one of its chapters.

It is the members of the project's National Assessment Team, however, who are responsible for reconceiving the boundaries of this final publication. I am indebted to each of them for their intellectual engagement with the project, their counsel throughout the three years, and their professional and personal friendships. Carolyne Arnold, Pat Hutchings, Lee Knefelkamp, Joan Poliner Shapiro, Jill Mattuck Tarule, and Mary Kay Thompson Tetreault first met as a group in October of 1989. During that breakfast meeting, an excited conversation was initiated that eventually transformed the idea for a rather pedestrian manual into the current volume. While we hope that the final version has lost none of its practical applications, we also have sought to insert a conceptual framework about assessment, feminist theory, and student learning.

In *A Room of One's Own*, Virginia Woolf insists, "A good dinner is of great importance to good talk. One cannot think well, love well, sleep well, if one has not dined well." Our conversation about feminist assessment began over a meal three years ago. We hope our collective efforts since then generate additional animated exchanges among diverse readers. There is an urgent need for those of us in higher education to talk candidly together about what our goals are as educators, how we can evaluate learning, and how students can be central to that investigative process. With an aim to initiating some of those dialogues, we offer this entree.

Caryn McTighe Musil
Project Director
Senior Research Associate, AAC

PART ONE

CONTEXTS
AND
CLIMATES

CHAPTER ONE

■

RELAXING YOUR NECK MUSCLES
THE HISTORY OF THE PROJECT
BY CARYN McTIGHE MUSIL

"You're advising me to do what? An assessment grant on women's studies?" My voice grew thinner. The muscles in my neck tightened. I managed to feign a certain modicum of interest. This was, after all, a FIPSE program officer I was speaking to. She had called that morning to give me feedback about a proposal I wanted to submit to the Fund for the Improvement of Postsecondary Education. The more she talked, the more my neck muscles tightened.

The voice on the end of the line suggested that given the increasingly contentious national debate about higher education, it would be instructive to examine women's studies programs more systematically in order to assess their contribution to student learning. Although I refrained from expressing it, I felt an overwhelming resistance to what proved to be very good advice.

My resistance was rooted in two things. The first was the weariness I felt, after nearly twenty years, from having to prove the value of women's studies one more time to a skeptical audience. The second was the negative associations the word "assessment" conjured up for me as a humanities professor. Assessment reminded me of the statistics course I never took, the computer programming course that was not available in my graduate days, and my deep suspicion that most quantitative analysis flattened out the more interesting things to be learned about education. I also thought of assessment as something that is done to you, frequently by external agencies with highly suspect motives. Paralyzed by my unfamiliarity with the expertise I thought one had to have to "do" assessment, for more than a week I was unable to write a single word of my grant proposal.

Feeling the imperative of a FIPSE deadline driving me, however, I began to investigate assessment. After reading extensively in the assessment literature and consulting nationally with assessment experts, I began to understand the range of debate in the field as well as the enormous variety of methods—both quantitative and qualitative—for collecting data. I realized that assessment could indeed generate invaluable data about women's studies and student learning that would answer questions not only for skeptics but also for women's studies professors.

Instead of a judgmental tool for punishment, assessment increasingly appeared as a source of illumination—the beginning, as Pat Hutchings of the American Association for Higher Education (AAHE) likes to put it, of a more informed conversation about teaching and student learning. Since the image of an animated conversation over time is an apt one for women's studies itself, describing assessment in those same terms made it seem commensurate with our own educational goals.

My own transformation from cool wariness about assessment to warmly embracing its possibilities paralleled the transformation I was to witness among the various participants during our three-year project. I recognized immediately the hesitancy and long list of questions that women's studies faculty members brought to our first workshop three years ago. As they themselves became assessment proponents, they began to describe the initial skepticism they encountered back at their campuses. In their final reports, however, faculty members at most sites commented how professors and students alike shifted their attitudes about assessment during the project's span. By sharing the process through which many of us moved from resisting to respecting assessment, we hope that *Students at the Center: Feminist Assessment* will become for its readers a vehicle that enhances campus conversations and ultimately expands what we know about what and how students learn.

WHY SUCH A BOOK NOW?

The larger context for the current educational climate of accountability is the global geo-political climate in which there is renewed pressure in the United States to demonstrate to the world—and to our own citizens—that we are still a superpower. There is an aroma of decline that frightens policy makers and citizens alike. This is especially true with regard to how the United States competes in trade and manufacturing, the quality of our products, and the productivity and creativity of our labor force. There is a fear that our powers are waning like other former imperial powers—England, France, the Soviet Union—despite our momentary triumphant euphoria when communist governments collapsed in the Soviet Union and Eastern Europe. In such an atmosphere of critical concern about what is happening to America, there is heated debate about what has caused this decline, who is to blame, and how to fix it.

As students from other countries—especially from our economic competitors—outperform U.S. students on standardized tests, our education systems have come under new scrutiny. In the more generalized call for educational reform that began in the 1980s and continues today, the earliest critique was aimed at elementary and secondary schools; the critique of higher education came later. The latter examination reveals concern about the content of the curriculum; the performance of students; the preparation of teachers and professors; the perceived decline in standards; the fragmentary nature of the curriculum; and the impact all this might be or already is having on the quality of college educated workers in the United States.

Several questions are contested: Who will set standards for what is excellent? Are such standards even possible? How do you measure them? What ought the role of federal, state, and local governments be in terms of accountability? What kind of knowledge do students need for their personal lives as well as their work lives? Who is not served well by our current educational systems? How do we create more affirming learning environments for diverse students?

What the "Courage to Question" project attempts to do is offer some solutions for an educational system in a moment of crisis and transition. Student bodies have changed radically in their typical profile: in terms of sex, race, and age; in terms of how and how long people move through the system; and in terms of the delivery systems created to reach this widely diverse student population—an increasing majority of whom commute to their classes or take those college classes at their workplace, the local Y, or the neighborhood elementary school. The content of the curriculum is hotly contested and altering even in the midst of adamant arguments that it should remain unchanged. The debate about content is complicated by the knowledge explosion that has occurred in this second half of the twentieth century, manifesting itself at the college level in a dramatic expansion in the number of courses, programs, and areas of inquiry. In the face of such a panoply of possibilities, content no longer is the easy vehicle providing intellectual coherence. Many argue we should be looking more at *how* students know rather than concentrating so fixedly on *what* they know. Finally, in a world where most students will change jobs at least four times in their working lives and might, in fact, be employed in jobs we have not even imagined, what preparation do they need as undergraduates to function in a pluralistic society deeply interconnected with the rest of the globe?

In the midst of all these questions and debates, what do we know about student learning? What can students tell us about what they need, what has worked, and how their lives have been changed by what happens during the college years? Our project turns to students to give us some answers, solicit-

We are urging that students be central to the
assessment process, that they be asked to reflect
about their learning, and that we listen and
record those narratives over time

ing student opinions in a variety of ways. Some people today are advocating
some sort of standardized "instrument of instruments" that can generate
indisputable national score sheets against which we can all measure our
individual and collective failures and successes. Our project sees such an approach as ineffectual. It stifles solutions rather than generating them. It offers
simple answers where only complex ones will suffice. Most significantly, it
creates a false sense of what the process of learning is all about.

This is not to say that there are no insights to be gained from measuring
things in statistical ways. It is not to argue against evaluation, defining areas
for improvement, or coming to some consensus on a variety of goals we hold
in common about the purpose of our educational enterprise. It is to suggest,
however, that there is no single goal, no single solution, no single measurement relevant to all.

In such a contentious climate, we are offering some space for collegial dialogue: among faculty members; among students; between faculty members
and students; among graduates; and among graduates, faculty members, and
current students. We are advocating a context-specific set of questions to be
asked and a context-specific set of means for gathering information to illuminate those questions. We are urging that students be central to the assessment
process, that they be asked to reflect about their learning, and that we listen
and record those narratives over time. We are joining with those who say it is
time to ask some hard questions—time to muster the courage to question
even things we might hold very dear. And we are especially interested in evidence that students possess the courage to question, which is so fundamental
to sustaining a vibrant, innovative society responsive to its citizens.

WOMEN'S STUDIES:
INSTITUTIONALIZATION AND BACKLASH

In 1989, the year the proposal for "The Courage to Question: Women's
Studies and Student Learning" was submitted to FIPSE, two events were occurring simultaneously that affected the shape of the grant and the attitudes
of many of us involved in the project. The first was the ongoing national call
for educational reform already mentioned, and the second was a national
plan to celebrate twenty years of institutionalized women's studies programs.
By 1988 and 1989, the call for educational reform was acquiring a distinctly
ideological edge; figures such as Secretary of Education William Bennett
lambasted faculty members for caving in to "special interests" such as wom-
en's studies and ethnic studies, and National Endowment for the Humanities

Chairman Lynne V. Cheney advocated returning to an American past un-clouded by what she perceived as "political" and intrusive distractions of race and gender.

Allan Bloom's *The Closing of the American Mind* (1987) extended Bennett's attack on campuses by arguing that all the problems in higher education today could be traced to the radical reformers of the 1960s, the es-tablishment of special programs like Black Studies—from which women's studies later modeled itself—and the decision to democratize academic insti-tutional structures. In 1989, the National Association of Scholars (NAS), a vociferous conservative group organized to stem progressive reforms, held its first national conference, which—despite attracting only two hundred par-ticipants—was covered on page two of *The Washington Post*. The National Women's Studies Association's (NWSA) national conference, held just up the road in Baltimore a few months later, drew more than two thousand par-ticipants but received no coverage whatsoever in the *Post*.

George Bush had been elected the "Education President" the year before and joined others insisting that educational excellence could be achieved if, among other things, we created the correct national test for measuring it. In 1989, he called for an Educational Summit of Governors, many of whom al-ready were working with their state legislatures to institute mandatory assess-ment of public schools and state-supported higher education institutions. Accountability was the rallying cry, global competitiveness in the market-place was the overwhelming driving force, and shrinking economic resources cloaked all of these initiatives with a punitive taint.

In the midst of this backlash, I—then executive director of NWSA—was planning an invitational conference for women's studies directors to mark two decades since the first program had been formally approved. The conference was designed to celebrate past achievements and forge an agenda for women's studies in the 1990s. Held in Washington, D.C., it drew almost double the number of participants in the NAS conference. NAS had titled its first confer-ence "Reclaiming the Academy," which explained in part why we in women's studies were celebrating and a small contingent of conservative academics were organizing. There was no question that our presence had made a differ-ence in the curriculum, in faculty and staffing, and in campus life.

While we sought to take pride in the difficult intellectual and political accomplishments of the previous two decades, we had few illusions that we were, as our critics liked to portray us, "running the universities." We under-stood better than they that we had indeed become institutionalized within

Women's studies teachers continue to be subject
to accusations that they are politicizing the
curriculum by including women and gender in their
courses, while those who exclude women are not

---

academia, but we also knew that we had little more than a toehold in many
places. Today there are 621 women's studies programs, but many are under-
staffed, underfunded, and housed in basements. Faculty members teach their
women's studies courses and invest hours in cocurricular programming often
with little reward from their institutions. Women's studies teachers continue
to be subject to accusations that they are politicizing the curriculum by including women and gender in their courses, while those who exclude women
are not.

Nonetheless, we understood that feminist scholarship had made it im-
possible to return to the unexamined biases of earlier years. Twenty years of
feminist scholarship had transformed many disciplines. Curricular transformation efforts had produced not only thousands of women's studies courses
but thousands more courses that integrated new scholarship about women
and gender into general education and the curriculum as a whole. New faculty lines in women's studies were becoming more common—a fact that in-
sured curricular stability. In addition to the unwavering growth in the
number of undergraduate women's studies programs, more of them were
establishing majors and minors. Moreover, what already had happened at the
undergraduate level was being replicated at the graduate level as concentra-
tions in women's studies, specializations within disciplinary degrees, and the
emergence of full master's programs in women's studies became evident by
the decade's end.

The most powerful witness to the influence of women's studies, however,
was the number of students attracted to it. Despite a period in the 1980s
when the national climate was largely unsympathetic to feminist concerns,
students continued to flock to women's studies courses. Those students were
women of all colors and ages who represented an increasing range of political
orientations. Men, too, began to take more of the courses, especially as they
became exposed to the new scholarship on women and gender through their
transformed general-education courses and electives. From those students we
continued to hear women's studies described as intellectually rigorous, personally transforming, dynamic in its teaching, and challenging in its insis-
tence that students integrate what they learned from courses into the choices
they make about how to live their daily lives.

FRAMEWORKS FOR THE GRANT

I was poised, then, between two tensions as I constructed the FIPSE assessment grant, "The Courage to Question: Women's Studies and Student

Learning." Women's studies was both embattled and triumphant: attacked by some as the reason for the current crisis in education, yet confident that it possessed some insights about how to remedy some of those crises. It was a time when we in women's studies were weary of having to justify our new courses, our tenure-line requests, our scholarship, our existence. But it was also a time to pause after twenty years of sustained activity and examine more systematically what the effects of all our program building were on student learning. At this historical juncture, more than anything else, we needed time for reflection.

The project's title, "The Courage to Question," was inspired by a student who claimed, "Women's studies gave me courage." Challenged by her words, I wanted us to enter full force into the national debate and see if we had such courage ourselves—courage to question whether we actually did what we said we were doing. Courage to question whether some of our critics might be right about us. Courage to listen to what our students were telling us about our courses, our teaching, our programmatic outreach. And finally, courage to go public with what we discovered, even if it might be used negatively by people unsympathetic to women's studies.

The grant, then, sought to assess questions fundamental to us in women's studies. We wanted to ask whether women's studies courses provide a dynamic interactive environment, encourage critical thinking, empower students as learners, enrich their sense of civilization's rich and diverse heritage, connect their knowledge from other courses, and challenge them to become actively engaged in shaping their world.

From the outset, there were some basic assumptions undergirding the design of the grant that were crucial to its success as an assessment grant. The evolution and refinement of those assumptions are discussed in more detail elsewhere in this book. From the beginning, it was understood that the assessment designs would be institution specific and that each program would have the responsibility for determining what questions it wanted to explore and how. All participants knew they were to use multiple measures to gather data and that those measures might include both quantitative and qualitative methods. There also was the expectation that the process would involve campus-wide consultations with faculty members and students as well as the national consultations, which the two representatives from each institution would have with two dozen other faculty members at our project meetings. Finally, there was an assumption that we needed a "National Assessment Team" of experts, familiar both with women's studies and with a variety of evaluation approaches, who could instruct project participants in assessment methods. Implicit in our design was the belief that, like our students, faculty members could be empowered as learners and anyone could be taught to "do" assessment in their courses.

In selecting the NATs—as they came to be known—there was a deliberate attempt to create a group of assessors with diverse yet complementary kinds of expertise. Combining scholars of learning and teaching with researchers who focused on diverse assessment techniques and methodology, the NATs could offer campus participants a wealth of approaches to evaluate student learning. It also was important to the success of the grant that the NATs not only were experts in assessment but also familiar with the interdisciplinary area of women's studies. Ultimately, these assessment consultants became the authors of the various chapters in *Students at the Center*. For a fuller description of each National Assessment Team member, see the "Directory of Consultants" at the end of this volume. The team included the following people:

♦ **Carolyne W. Arnold,** a senior researcher from the Wellesley Research Center for Women and an assistant professor of sociology at the University of Massachusetts–Boston, has expertise in quantitative assessment with a special emphasis on minority women and public health.

♦ **Pat Hutchings,** a senior research associate at the American Association for Higher Education and former director of AAHE's Assessment Forum, has a national overview of what is being done in assessment and which approaches have revealed the most.

♦ **Lee Knefelkamp,** chair of the Higher Education Department at Columbia University's Teachers College, has written and lectured widely about students' intellectual and ethical development and about different learning styles.

♦ **Joan Poliner Shapiro**, associate dean at Temple University's College of Education and formerly co-director of the Women's Studies Program at the University of Pennsylvania, uses both quantitative and qualitative assessment approaches in her area of expertise: feminist assessment.

♦ **Jill Mattuck Tarule**, dean of the College of Education and Social Services at the University of Vermont, uses qualitative research and formative evaluation to trace developmental themes, especially concerning women as learners.

♦ **Mary Kay Thompson Tetreault,** dean of the School of Human Development and Community Service at California State University–Fullerton, is known for her work on feminist pedagogy and curriculum development and most recently has used an ethnographic approach to analyze teaching.

In communicating to the public what it had discovered, the project had at least two stories that needed to be told. The first concerned the actual research findings of the seven participating colleges and universities. That volume of case studies became *The Courage to Question: Women's Studies and Student Learning*, which was followed by the publication of a twelve-page *Executive Summary*. The second story that needed to be told was not about the findings themselves but about the process that led to them.

Students at the Center is a hybrid of a typical assessment manual. We wanted a "how" and a "why" assessment book, not just a "how to." We have thus retained the practical value of collecting sample questionnaires, alumnae/i surveys, strategies for focus groups, bibliographies, a directory of campus consultants, and other such useful information. We also have sought to include a more theoretical and historical framework. Would something evolve out of this project that we could call feminist assessment? What would its governing principles be? What is the relation of feminist assessment to the broader assessment movement? What kinds of approaches and methodologies would our project create? How would they compare with the range of alternatives used by any number of evaluators? Were there new questions that women's studies people would pose about assessment? What were the political implications for women's studies to participate in such a project? What use would be made of the findings? by whom? for what purposes? What were the particular sources of greatest resistance to assessment in women's studies, and what might we learn by being attentive to those resistances?

The chapters, while individually authored, are the result of an ongoing three-year conversation about the topic among the seven of us. It is a conversation that has occurred during formal meetings with National Assessment Team members, conference calls, and papers prepared for panel presentations over the life of the project. Our conversations also have assumed the form of short written exchanges about focused issues as we conceived the shape of *Students at the Center*.

As we debated a title for our assessment book, we kept coming back to what we thought distinguished "The Courage to Question" as a project. It was, at heart, student-centered. At each campus, students, for the most part, were involved in every level of inquiry: in the formulation of program goals and of key questions to investigate and in supplying the data on which the case studies rest. On several campuses, students became central investigators with women's studies faculty members.

Although it was published after we had already picked our title, Jean O'Barr's and Mary Wyer's *Engaging Feminism: Student Speak Up and Speak Out* captures eloquently the way we in higher education do not listen carefully enough to students. Because of our inattention, we have overlooked one of our richest resources: students themselves.

> It is all well and good to suggest that students might learn from each other.... It is even acceptable to say that...we should learn with students, cooperating with them in a common classroom ac-tivity. It is another issue altogether to suggest that those teaching in American higher education today, including those in women's studies, would be enriched by a shift in our perspectives on stu-dents, to suggest that we might be more effective teachers if our approach was grounded in an appreciation for the knowledge, di-versity, and intellectual strengths of those who take our classes. If we listen to what these students...say, they thrive on recogni-tion, appreciation, and trust; they notice their marginalization; and they despair of the waste of their talents.[1]

Sharing O'Barr's and Wyer's desire to refocus new attention to students' voic-es, especially as we assess the strengths and weaknesses of the education they are subjected to for so many years, we titled our book *Students at the Center: Feminist Assessment*.

THE STRUCTURE OF THE GRANT

Ten women's studies programs were invited to be part of the project. Seven ended up completing all three years. The grant was structured around a series of workshops with two representatives from each campus, the National Assessment Team members, and the project director. The first year focused on defining campus-based program goals in consultation with broad campus constituencies, determining what key areas they wanted to investigate about student learning, and designing an assessment plan for their program. During the second year, programs put their plans into practice—gathering data, bringing National Assessment Team members to campus for site visits, and writing preliminary reports of their findings. In the third year, final data col-lection and analysis were completed and final chapters of the findings writ-ten for *The Courage to Question: Women's Studies and Student Learning*, published in June 1992.

At the beginning of the project, each campus was asked to define its women's studies program goals in four areas: the knowledge base, critical skills, feminist pedagogy, and personal growth. There were, however, no pre-conceived formulas for program goals and no assumption that they would be the same at each campus. We did assume, nonetheless, that once they were compiled we all would gain a more accurate picture of what women's studies learning goals were across the nation. With this task as the focus of the first year of the project, yet another given of the grant proposal surfaced: nothing was permanent, nothing was sacred, and, like most women, we could change our minds.

The first year of the project began with a workshop in October, 1989, tied to the invitational women's studies directors' conference, "Women's Studies: The Third Decade." Participants gathered around the table for that workshop arrived with all the recognizable signs of caution, resistance, and suspicion about assessing women's studies that had surfaced for me during my first phone conversation with FIPSE.

Central to the work of the first year was articulating on each campus what we came to call "passionate questions." The phrase builds on the use of "passionate" in *Women's Ways of Knowing*, where the concept of "passionate knowers" is defined as "a way of weaving their passions and intellectual life into some recognizable whole."[2] They are described as "knowers who enter into a union with that which is to be known."[3] We urged students and faculty and staff members on campuses to become "passionate questioners," focusing on issues of greatest concern, without worrying until later about how to answer them. The decision to focus squarely on questions of great importance provided an overriding purpose for the project and gave us the impetus to plunge ahead. Passionate anxieties began to give way to passionate questions.

By the spring of that first year, campus representatives had accumulated an expanded set of questions spawned by several months of consultation with faculty members and students. Although we debated whether to have a common set of questions to ask across all campuses, we decided against such an approach. Instead, we remained firm in our premise that positionality and institutional context should determine the specific questions posed for each of the women's studies programs involved. "I like to keep things messy," said one women's studies faculty member who was explaining her distrust of pre-determined questions and categories. Generating the questions proved the most important part of the process. As Mary Kay Tetreault, one of the National Assessment Team members, put it, "Being clear about what you

'Being clear about what you want to know is the
hard part; measuring that is easier'

---

want to know is the hard part. Measuring that is easier."

One of the greatest obstacles during the first year was wariness toward
the assessment movement and its language. We devoted many discussions
to assessment: its uses and misuses, its range of methods, its value, and its
potential as a vehicle we could claim as our own. Had the programs not
ultimately decided that they could, in fact, create a version of assessment
consistent with feminist goals and maintain some control about how the results would be used, the project would not have lasted beyond the first six
months. Faculty members at Hunter College described the gradual transformation in their attitudes this way: "Learning about assessment as a tool for
curricular improvement, and not as a means of disciplining the faculty and
student workforce, has been extremely valuable."

Through articles circulated to participants, group discussions, campus-
wide consultations, and one-on-one meetings with members of the National
Assessment Team, participants gradually made their peace with assessment.
Although most resistance to assessment had been overcome, the residue remained in the reluctance to call their design an "assessment plan." We eventually settled for "The Institutional Research Design Assessment Plan."
While IRDAP sounded more like a new weapons system than an investigation of student learning, it was language everyone could live with.

The difficulty most programs faced as they were about to launch their
assessment investigations was captured succinctly by one women's studies
director: "Where is this going to fit in when nothing else has dropped out?"
People worried there was no time, no staff, and few resources. On some campuses, the project was not a program priority for everyone. We tried to solve
these problems by pressing for more institutional support in the form of released time, research assistants, and developmental funds. In some cases we
were successful; in others the failure to get more institutional cooperation
created insurmountable difficulties for some sites and slowed others considerably. We urged creative use of staff time by weaving the assessment plan into
a seminar project for a women's studies major, a student internship, or a graduate student research project. That proved a very successful strategy for several programs.

We also urged programs to pick a plan they could actually do, maintaining consonance between resources and ambition. We recommended an unobtrusive assessment strategy to embed the questions in what programs
already do on campus. Once they had gathered the data, we reminded them
that they needed only to ask *some* of the questions at this point and could re-

turn to the data later when time and staffing permitted.

These various strategies did not solve every problem, but they gave programs momentum and confidence. As one participant described it, our workshop offered a reality check on what programs can accomplish and "helped check overambitious plans. The workshop provided me again with a sense of purpose, importance, and enthusiasm. All of the earlier reservations vanished as each campus got down to business."

The efforts during the second year took place primarily on individual campuses where programs collected all sorts of data through a wide variety of methods. Some used focus interviews; others examined student journals over time; still others used surveys, pre- and post-tests, reviewed syllabi, observed classes, examined annual reports, and phoned alumnae and alumni. On several campuses, students were deeply involved in collecting data, analyzing it, and writing up reports. On most campuses, a significant number of faculty members became increasingly part of the process. The most recurrent problem during the second year was knowing what to do with the mountain of data that was now available about student learning in women's studies. National Assessment Team members made site visits and offered telephone consultations to help unravel this dilemma.

Throughout the first and second years, and even into the third and final year of the grant, the project benefitted significantly because everyone was so willing to share what they knew and did. While the grant structured such a process into the design, the sites entered into the exchange with relish. Everyone had a copy of each other's program goals and institutional profiles. We compared our "passionate questions" and paired in different clusters to help each other formulate assessment designs, which also were shared with everyone in the project. Programs exchanged course evaluations, alumnae surveys, and classroom climate surveys already in use. This level of exchange, intense dialogue, and mutual support contributed to the project's eventual success.

By the end of the second year, the seven participating programs wrote their preliminary reports, revealing among other things the importance of engaging in assessment. As Marcia Westkott of the University of Colorado put it when she compared our assessment project with the state's, "The state mandate created an atmosphere that encouraged compliance rather than enthusiasm." By the end of our project, faculty members and students had become passionate questioners in assessment, intellectually challenged through discussion with a women's studies national community, and informed in very concrete ways about some of the strengths and areas to improve in their programs. By the end of the project, every program had generated not only new insights about student learning but also a host of additional passionate questions to pose in their post-project lives. They had come full circle indeed.

Women's studies participants became convinced that student-centered, feminist assessment as they came to define it is a useful vehicle for improving teaching and learning in women's studies. In publishing this volume, our hope is that the conceptual shifts, strategies, and instruments we developed during our three-year experience will be useful to faculty members and administrators whether or not they teach in women's studies programs. We also hope that by the time you finish reading our book, the muscles in your neck will not tighten the next time you hear the word "assessment."

---

1. Jean O'Barr and Mary Wyer, eds., *Engaging Feminism: Students Speak Up & Speak Out* (Charlottesville, Va.: University Press of Virginia, 1992), 1.
2. Mary Field Belenky, Blythe McVicker Clinchy, Nancy Rule Goldberger, and Jill Mattuck Tarule, *Women's Ways of Knowing: The Development of Self, Voice, and Mind* (New York: Basic Books, 1986), 141.
3. *Ibid.*

CHAPTER TWO

■

THE ASSESSMENT MOVEMENT AND FEMINISM:
CONNECTION OR COLLISION?
BY PAT HUTCHINGS

NWSA's project, "The Courage to Question," is the story of what happens when two apparently very different educational movements collide. On the one hand, there is the women's studies movement, some twenty years old now and understood to have an overtly political agenda. On the other hand, there is the assessment movement, a more recent arrival on the scene dating back less than a decade. Assessment's agenda is not only less overtly political than that of women's studies, it is also perhaps harder to define since its purpose, methods, and practice on campuses have been characterized by considerable uncertainty, variety, and its own evolution. To understand how women's studies has both contributed to and benefitted from assessment, it is necessary to understand the fluid history of the assessment movement itself.

ASSESSMENT AND UNDERGRADUATE REFORM

Although the most salient feature of assessment for many campuses has been that it is mandated, there are in fact powerful ideas about *education* behind today's call for assessment. Ten years ago, Alexander Astin argued that traditional ways of thinking about quality in higher education—as a function of resources and reputation (high student SATs, faculty Ph.D.s, endowment, library holdings, and so forth)—told too little, even misled. Rather, Astin argued, the real measure of quality was found in a college's *results*, its *contribution to student learning*, the "value added" from the experiences it provided.

By the mid-1980s, this new view of quality had taken hold in an undergraduate reform movement growing within the academy and spearheaded by two influential reports. In late 1984, a National Institute of Education study panel (on which Astin sat) issued "Involvement in Learning," which argued that to strengthen learning one needed to involve students in their studies, set high expectations, and assess and provide feedback.[1] In early 1985, the Association of American Colleges' *Integrity in the College Curriculum* also made this learning/assessment link, calling it scandalous that colleges failed to assess the impacts of their teaching.[2]

Behind both reports lies a view that quality is indeed a function of student learning. And behind that view lies a set of questions that are at the

Many campuses undertook assessment begrudgingly at first. Uncertainty about state mandates [and] concerns about misuse of data ran high. Today, campuses report that assessment has made a positive difference

---

heart of today's assessment movement:
▶ What do the courses and instruction we provide add up to for students?
▶ What do our students know and what can they do?
▶ Are they learning what we think we are teaching?
▶ Does their achievement match what our degrees imply?
▶ How do we know and ensure that?
▶ How can the quantity and quality of student learning be improved?

These are hard questions—and important ones—in that they call up even more fundamental questions about the purposes of our educational programs and institutions. The good news is that over the past ten years of the assessment movement many campuses have taken these questions seriously and have become increasingly adept at answering them in useful ways.[3]

THE ASSESSMENT MOVEMENT

In the early 1980s, the number of institutions engaged in assessing student learning was just a handful: Alverno College, King's College (Penn.), Miami–Dade Community College, Northeast Missouri State University, and the University of Tennessee–Knoxville. What these campuses were doing and what they *meant* by assessment varied wildly—from attention to individual student learning at Alverno, for instance, to the collection of data to satisfy a state performance-funding formula in Tennessee.

Then, in 1987, came the report from the National Governors' Association (NGA), *Time for Results*, with a call from its Task Force on College Quality for the nation's colleges and universities to begin doing assessment.

The public has a right to know and understand the quality of undergraduate education that young people receive from publicly funded colleges.... They have a right to know that their resources are being wisely invested and committed.... We need not just more money for education, we need more education for the money.[4]

Assessment activities that had been developed at Alverno College over the previous decade were cited as a model for other campuses to follow. It was "time for results," and the presumption was that assessment would produce those results.

Not long after the NGA report came a series of state mandates requiring public colleges and universities to begin doing assessment and reporting results. Although the mandates and the motives behind them differed considerably, state after state jumped onto the assessment bandwagon to show their

seriousness about educational quality, to control costs, to enforce accountability, or to prompt improvement. By 1990, forty states (up from four or five
in the mid-1980s) had in place or in progress some kind of assessment initiative. Further incentives entered the picture in the fall of 1988, when the
U.S. Department of Education began to insist that accrediting bodies, regional and programmatic, require "information on student achievement"
(read: assessment) from the institutions and programs they accredited.

Today's higher-education landscape reflects the power of these external
mandates for assessment. According to a 1991 American Council on Education survey, 81 percent of colleges and universities report having some
form of assessment activity currently underway. Just over half of the public
institutions are working under a state mandate to develop a student assessment program, with eight in ten of these having already submitted required
data. Two-thirds say that assessment is part of a self-study for a regional accrediting agency. Notably, too, significant numbers of institutions are planning further assessment activities.[5]

THE EVOLUTION OF CAMPUS PRACTICE

As the amount of assessment activity has risen, so too has its character.
Many campuses undertook assessment begrudgingly at first. Uncertainty
about what to do in the face of new (and often unclear) state mandates, as
well as concerns about possible misuse of data, ran high. Today, however,
campuses report that assessment has made a positive difference. Fifty-two
percent of the nation's colleges and universities report that assessment has
led to changes in curricula or programs. Faculty members involved in assessment report that their view of teaching and their activities in the classroom
also have been affected. (Four in ten institutions estimate that more than 40
percent of faculty members have participated in assessment.) Elaine El-
Khawas of the American Council on Education summarizes: "Assessment has
had widespread early influence, growing over a few years' time to a point
where most institutions of higher education can see some impact of their assessment activities."[6]

One factor that has shaped the direction of assessment has been state-
level action. Earlier fears that states would roll out mandatory statewide tests
have not been borne out. Rather, two-thirds of the states chose to follow the
more permissive path charted by Virginia: Each public institution is to practice assessment in ways of its own choosing, consistent with its particular
mission and clientele, with required reports focused largely on evidence that

Assessment is *not* primarily an administrative task—it is an educational process

---

it has put findings to use in making improvements.

A second factor stems from a kind of invention by necessity. Many of the questions posed by assessment mandates could not, in fact, be answered by existing, commercially available instruments. The Educational Testing Service (ETS) and American College Testing (ACT) quickly rallied to the market demand with tests aimed at learning in general education and, subsequently, the major. Although many of those new instruments have become increasingly useful and relevant, they are not always a good match for campus curricula, and many campuses began inventing their own methods and approaches by necessity. As of 1991, 69 percent were developing their own instruments, an increase from 34 percent in 1988.

The good news here is that while assessment was initially seen by many as synonymous with an SAT- or ACT-like test, it now includes a wide range of faculty-designed approaches, many of which not only provide rich data but constitute educationally meaningful experiences for students. Portfolios in particular (a method employed by several of the programs participating in the "Courage to Question" project) have gained popularity, with 45 percent of institutions using them as part of an assessment venture by 1991. Looking at the program for the American Association for Higher Education's National Conference on Assessment in Higher Education for the past few years, one sees a wide range of rich methods, including focus groups, interviews, projects, capstone course activities, surveys of current students and graduates, transcript analysis, the use of external examiners, and student self-assessment.

In addition to a richer and more varied set of assessment methods, one now sees a more sophisticated *conception* of assessment. Many campuses have come to embrace a view of assessment that ties it firmly to learning and offers genuine hope for real undergraduate reform:

♦ *Focus on improving rather than proving.*
Because assessment arrived on many campuses as a state-mandated requirement, the need often was perceived as proving something to skeptical publics. That need is not without warrant, but campuses that have come to understand assessment as gathering and using information for internal improvement rather than for external proof have gotten further and to more interesting places faster.

♦ *Focus on student experience over time.*
The early focus of assessment tended to be "outcomes"—which is understandably what outside, policy-making audiences were most concerned about

and also what existing methods were most suited to. For purposes of improvement, however, campuses quickly found that they needed to know not only
outcomes but also the experiences and processes (teaching, curriculum, services, student effort, and the like) that led up to those outcomes.

♦ *Use multiple methods and sources of information.*
To understand what was behind these outcomes, clearly a single "snapshot"
approach to assessment would not be sufficient. As campus assessment programs have grown more sophisticated and comprehensive, a variety of methods have been adopted and invented to help provide the fullest possible
picture of what students are learning and how learning might be improved.
Tests may be used, but so are interviews with students, surveys of employers,
judgments by external examiners, and portfolios of student work over time.

♦ *Pay attention at the outset to issues of how information will be used.*
In assessment's early days, often with state-mandated deadlines just around
the corner, the rush to "get some information" was almost inevitable. Gradually, however, campuses have learned to think harder in advance about what
information will actually be helpful, to whom, and under what conditions.
Using assessment for improvement means focusing on significant, real
questions.

♦ *Provide occasions to talk about and interpret information.*
The gap between information and improvement is considerable; what is
needed to close it, many campuses have found, are occasions where faculty
members, administrators, students, and others can talk together about the
meaning of the information that assessment has made available. Is it good
news? Bad news? What action is implied? Where is improvement needed and
how should it be pursued?

♦ *Involve faculty members.*
Faculty members have long practice in making judgments about student
work; their expertise in doing so is crucial in deciding what questions assessment should focus on, what the data add up to, and what should be done to
improve. Since the single most important route to improvement is through
the classroom, faculty members in particular must be active participants in
the assessment process. Assessment is *not* primarily an administrative task—
it is an educational process.

♦ *Involve and listen to students.*
Assessment needs the information that students—and only students—can
provide. But *listening* to students is important ultimately because it is students' ability to assess themselves and to direct their own learning that will

Feminist assessment comes out of a fundamental commitment to the individual and her voice, her account of her own story, and a refusal to wash out individual or group differences

matter most. It is no accident that assessment was introduced to higher education in a report called *Involvement in Learning*.

FEMINIST ASSESSMENT

At first glance, feminist assessment looks much like the practice that has emerged on many campuses to this point. The principles of assessment enacted by the programs featured in this project are congruent with those (characterized by the previous list, for instance) that have evolved on many campuses where assessment is "working." What distinguishes feminist assessment, however, is the *way* these principles have been arrived at. Whereas many campus programs have been shaped largely by pragmatic concerns, feminist assessment is shaped by a coherent system of values and by feminist theory.

Consider, for instance, the shift away from multiple-choice tests. Faced with state mandates to assess the outcomes of general education, often with a pressing deadline, many campuses were quick to seize on new (or newly visible) instruments from the testing companies—ETS's Academic Profile and ACT's College Outcomes Measurement Program. What became increasingly clear, however, was that data from those tests—returned months later in a handful of subscores—shed little light on questions of improvement. What did it mean that students scored 76 percent on critical thinking? Was that good or bad? If bad, what should be changed? Even if the data had been more intrinsically useful—more connected to curricula and teaching—the chances of their being used were drastically diminished by general faculty contempt for such exams. As a result, many campuses now have minimized the role of such tests in a larger assessment program or actually dropped them from their current activities. What rules the day are more qualitative, faculty-driven approaches and a range of methods beyond tests.

Feminist assessment shares the view that standardized tests should play a minimal role in assessment. What is striking, however, is that the programs highlighted in "The Courage to Question" came to that conclusion not out of practical necessity but out of a view of learning itself and of knowledge. In a feminist view of the world, knowledge does not come in little boxes. Women's studies programs have considered it a given that learning is both about a subject *and* about how that subject might explain, influence, or make one's daily life choices easier, clearer, or more complex. It is assumed that what students learn in class will affect their lives outside of the class because gender is not contained by the walls of the classroom. Students may never see Egyptian art outside the slides shown in art history

class, but they will see some of the ways men and women or power and pow-
erlessness play out their complex dynamics elsewhere. They probably will
witness this in their first half hour after class. Relatedly, knowledge is not
purely objective but is understood to be socially constructed and "connected." This is not, clearly, a view of learning that makes multiple-choice tests
the method of choice.

The principle of student involvement provides a second illustration of
the distinctiveness of feminist assessment. Campuses that relied heavily on
commercially available tests administered as an add-on to regular academic
work quickly found themselves up against student motivation problems.
One campus sent letters to several thousand students who were scheduled to
take one of the multiple-choice exams then popular. Of the several thousand who received the letter, only thirty-some appeared. On other campuses, student participation was stimulated with free T-shirts, pizzas, and—in a
couple cases—with cash! Even where students were induced to show up,
however, motivation to do their best was clearly low, and cases of actual
sabotage (random filling in of the black dots) began to appear. All of this, of
course, made the "results" of such tests highly suspect and threw national
norming attempts into disarray. As a consequence, campus after campus
has realized that more useful assessment will result when students who are
invested in the process see that assessment matters—to them and to the
institution. One now sees more integral forms of assessment taking prece-
dence—often designed by faculty members and administered in courses,
sometimes required for graduation, and, on a few campuses, counting toward
grades.

Feminist assessment, too, takes student involvement in the assessment
process to be imperative. Students, as this book's title puts it, should be "at
the center." But that position stems not from an attempt to fix practical and
psychometric problems caused by low student motivation; feminist assessment is student-centered because of a theoretical, practical, and personal
commitment to women—and ultimately to all students—to how they learn
and thus to the things students themselves can tell us about how they learn.
Feminist assessment comes out of a fundamental commitment to the individual and her voice, her account of her own story, and a refusal to wash out individual or group differences.

In addition, it should be noted that feminism is the source of some of
the cautiousness about how assessment should be done. As feminists, we "locate ourselves" as questioners and skeptics since so much of what we have

I hope[d] that the kind of assessment women's studies programs would invent would make a lasting difference in the quality of undergraduate education; that is indeed what has happened

---

been told has turned out to be incomplete or distorted. We also assume there is politics underlying issues of knowledge, and it causes us to ask about the uses to which assessment will be put. Who has the power to determine the questions? What methods are most appropriate to embrace the many voices and ways of speaking? What methods help reveal the unspoken?

A FINAL REFLECTION

At the outset of "The Courage to Question," Caryn McTighe Musil asked me if I would be involved in the project. I was pleased to do so because I am committed to women's studies and intrigued by the possibility of more systematic information about the kinds of learning that go on in such programs. As I told Caryn, however, the eagerness of my response also was largely a function of a *hope*—a hope that the kind of assessment women's studies programs would invent would be precisely the kind that I had become persuaded, in my role as director of the AAHE Assessment Forum, could make a lasting difference in the quality of undergraduate education.

That, in my view, is indeed what has happened. The general assessment movement and the women's studies movement have intersected at several very productive points. Much more is said about these points in subsequent chapters, but one sees, for instance, the interest in multiple measures that has come to characterize the assessment movement more generally now bolstered by women's studies' commitment to multiple voices. Assessment's focus on student experience over time both has informed and been enhanced by a commitment to the authority of experience as a source of knowledge in feminist assessment and classrooms. In both the general assessment movement and in feminist assessment, the need to involve faculty members and students has been clear. Feminist assessment has pushed this principle further yet by examining and questioning the very nature of the classroom experience and the essential teacher-student relationship.

No doubt feminist assessment will continue to evolve, as will assessment more generally. My hope is that this volume will contribute to developments in both areas and that we will see a new infusion of energy and direction out of the ways of thinking about students, learning, and pedagogy that characterize the assessment work that has now come to pass in the programs featured here.

1. *Involvement in Learning: Realizing the Potential of American Higher Education*, Final Report of the Study Group on the Condition of Excellence in American Higher Education (Washington: National Institute of Education, 1984).

2. *Integrity in the College Curriculum* (Washington: Association of American Colleges, 1985).

3. Much of my thinking about assessment in general grows out of long conversations with my colleague, Ted Marchese, at AAHE. See especially the article "Watching Assessment: Questions, Stories, Prospects," co-authored with Ted Marchese, in *Change 22* (September/October 1990).

4. *Time for Results: The Governors' 1991 Report on Education* (Washington: National Governors' Association Center for Policy Research and Analysis, 1986).

5. Elaine El-Khawas, *Campus Trends, 1991*, Higher Education Panel Reports, No. 81 (Washington: American Council on Education, 1991).

6. Ibid., 15.

PART TWO

FEMINIST THEORY
AND
ASSESSMENT

CHAPTER THREE

■

WHAT IS FEMINIST ASSESSMENT?

BY JOAN POLINER SHAPIRO

Although the central focus of "The Courage to Question" was to investigate exactly what and how students were learning in women's studies classes, another fascinating area of inquiry appeared simultaneously. The parallel narrative that emerged involved the *process* that faculty members and students eventually adopted for gathering information about student learning in their programs. It was a story that members of the National Assessment Team (NATs) and the project director began to record from the very first time they met as a group in the fall of 1989. While there was no question that the primary function of the National Assessment Team was to instruct faculty members in assessment theories, strategies, and methods, its ancillary function was to formulate some broad-based principles about feminist assessment growing from the evaluative process itself on the different campuses.

In an early session, the NATs determined that there would be different forms of assessment on each site rather than a standard form of measurement. The women's studies and gender studies program directors concurred. They and the NATs judged that the context would drive the assessment criteria. We all felt that, if provided a wealth of diverse assessment approaches, women's studies faculty members and students would select methods appropriate for their particular site. It also was thought that, given the common knowledge base of feminist scholarship, feminist pedagogy, and feminist research methodology, there would be enough similarities discovered in the assessment process and products without the need for a standard instrument.

Workshops were held by the NATs that presented a range of diverse forms of assessment. The measures and techniques introduced included:
► institutional profile data
► historical document analysis
► student evaluation of courses
► surveys (structured and unstructured)
► portfolios
► individual interviews and/or group ones (collective conversations)
► journals, individual and/or group (a dialogic journal)
► self-assessment

Feminist assessment turns to students to reveal
what is important to *them*, what *they* want to
learn, and where *their* needs are not being met

- ▶ performance assessment
- ▶ feminist classroom observations (sometimes compared with regular classroom observations)
- ▶ course syllabi analysis.

For the purposes of validity, different forms of triangulation were used to assess this project. According to Sharon Merriam, triangulation means "using multiple investigators, multiple sources of data, or multiple methods to confirm the emerging findings."[1] Multiple measures for assessment were deemed important to provide one form of triangulation. Program directors, their faculty members, and students chose from the array of approaches and techniques the kinds of assessment appropriate for their sites. Their choices were very much guided by the resources available to them on a given campus—extra help to carry out the assessment process, released time provided or not provided, administrative support for women's studies, and the political realities of the site.

Another form of triangulation used in this study focused on multiple perspectives, and it therefore became important to hear diverse voices. Participants on a given site took into account as many of the voices—of students, of faculty members, of administrators, and of alumnae/i—as were applicable for their context. While the focus was on what students learned in women's studies or gender studies classrooms, varied perspectives for understanding the learning environment were deemed essential.

GUIDING FEMINIST
ASSESSMENT PRINCIPLES

The guiding principles of feminist assessment that emerged by the completion of this three-year project are outgrowths of what has been learned from the perspectives of the NATs, the project director, and the participating programs. These principles emerged from the accumulated data and observations emanating from the diverse women's studies and gender studies programs. These nine principles are meant to be a provisionary guide to conducting feminist assessment; they summarize our major ideas on this new area of assessment thus far.

It is important to note that in defining the following guiding principles, the terms "assessment" and "evaluation" often are used interchangeably. This is because the approaches to evaluation that are most compatible with feminist pedagogy and assessment frequently are those that are non-traditional and involve an emphasis on the process rather than the product. These approaches tend to focus on the improvement of instruction and the development of a positive learning environment on a particular site, rather than stressing cross-site comparisons for accountability purposes. They tend to recognize not only the voice of an evaluator but also the voices of others—such as participants and program directors—who have been a part of the process.

♦ *Principle 1: Feminist assessment questions almost everything related to evaluation.*

As the title of the project—"The Courage to Question"—suggests, feminist assessment questions almost everything that is related to evaluation. Feminist assessment is open to questioning how assessment previously has been carried out, including all paradigms, traditions, approaches, and instruments. It raises questions about methodology, purposes, power, use, politics, and the social context. It may ultimately find that the answers to its questions will ally feminist assessment with other "schools" or paradigms for assessment. However, we begin by assuming that what has been done before probably is inadequate—and often inadequate because it has not posed enough questions to see power relations, to note who is missing from the discussion, to appreciate the importance of context, and to understand the need to cross paradigms or to recognize shifting paradigms for purposes of assessment.

♦ *Principle 2: Feminist assessment is student-centered.*

Feminist assessment, when tied to student learning, is dependent on students for information about what they are learning. This approach is in marked contrast to other methods tradionally used in assessment. For example, the national report *America 2000* relies on the creation of national tests in which students must perform to meet someone else's preconceived determination of what is valuable.[2] By contrast, feminist assessment turns to students to reveal what is important to *them*, what *they* want to learn, and where *their* needs are not being met. In feminist assessment, student involvement in evaluating their own learning is a guiding principle. Students may serve as the key source of information, as participants in the research process itself, and—in some cases—as co-assessors with faculty members.

Feminist assessment recognizes there is no single student who can possibly stand for the whole. In keeping with its theoretical suspicion of aggregates and universals that too often have obscured women as a group or women in our particularity—such as women of color, women with disabilities, older women, or lesbians—feminist assessment pays attention to the distinctiveness of the individual learner. It also looks for possible and more

Our concept of assessment moves more from the
'inside out' rather than from the 'outside in'

informative patterns emerging from smaller disaggregate groupings. Since the standpoint from which each of us views the world leads inevitably toward partial perspectives, feminist assessment gains its power from holding on as much as possible to the insights of those partial perspectives, forming in the process a more textured and accurate collective whole.

♦ **Principle 3: Feminist assessment is participatory.**
Grounded in feminist theory—which seeks to understand oppressive silencing—and in feminist pedagogy—which seeks to give students voice—feminist assessment is deeply committed to an interactive strategy that generates a rich conversation. Less like an external process imposed by detached and distanced experts, feminist assessment resembles more a group of people gathered together to create meaning. As such, it opens up the process rather than narrowing its options and opinions. Those involved in the project (consultants, project personnel, researchers, students) form different configurations throughout the study, and their roles continue to be in flux. In "The Courage to Question," consultants, for example, often changed roles and became learners during joint planning sessions or in their visits to the various sites; students frequently became the assessors of their own learning process. In these ways, traditional hierarchical patterns and power relationships are challenged.

Such participatory evaluation emphasizes that those who will be assessed should be part of a continuing dialogue related to the evaluative process. Each participant is encouraged to have a voice in the evaluative process. Participatory evaluation[3]—an offshoot of illuminative evaluation[4]—combines both qualitative and quantitative evaluative methods and is designed specifically with women's studies and non-traditional programs in mind.

This participatory approach to assessment has been very much the case in our current study. Inherent in this project has been the underlying assumption that program directors, faculty members, and students on each campus should determine how student learning would best be assessed at their individual sites. Participants also knew at the outset that they would be expected to play an active role in the selection of evaluative techniques, collection and analysis of data, and writing the final report.

♦ **Principle 4: Feminist assessment is deeply affected by its context or institutional culture.**
While much traditional research decontextualizes its inquiries and findings, feminist assessment is informed continually by context. It therefore avoids abstractions that are not understood to be firmly rooted in a specific time, place, or history. For women's studies or gender studies programs, the context

or institutional culture is important and cannot be ignored, particularly when the delicate area of assessing student learning is what is being measured. On certain campuses, the women's studies or gender studies program is an integral part of the institution, while on others it may be more marginal. At some sites, feminism may be seen as subversive and dangerous; at another it may be considered a cutting-edge area. It is clear that the kind of assessment that can be carried out on a particular site is affected by the political realities of the institution—and our political realities of the culture at large. In short, *the politics of assessment* looms large in this area of feminist assessment.

Additionally, the contextual reality of an urban, suburban, or rural campus can create a very different program. For example, an urban campus might have a very diverse student population, while a rural campus might be homogeneous in its student composition. Further, geographical locations can lead to the development of unique programs. In the U.S., a southwestern program may emphasize Native American women, while a northeastern program may focus on the study of Latina and African-American women. *Hence, a site-specific assessment process becomes important to measure student learning in different contexts or institutional cultures.*

♦ *Principle 5: Feminist assessment is decentered.*

Feminist assessment begins to deconstruct the usual "outside-in" or stringent vertical hierarchy to create a more open, varied, and web-like structure. It avoids an "outsider" or more dominant, powerful, and seemingly objective force determining what questions should be asked and how they should be framed. It also avoids an attempt to meet some abstract notion of excellence that has no roots or connections to the group, program, or curriculum being evaluated.

Our concept of assessment moves more from the "inside out" rather than from the "outside in." In this project, while a structure was built into the assessment process, the structure provided for different loci of power. A "neutral" outside assessor was not envisioned. Instead, many knowledgeable inside assessors (NATs, project director, program directors, faculty members, students) were utilized who were conversant with the pedagogy, methodology, and scholarship under review and who were active in the design and development of the assessment process.

♦ *Principle 6: Feminist assessment approaches should be compatible with feminist activist beliefs.*

Feminist assessment is driven by its immediate connection to the implications of its research. That is, feminist assessment expects its thinking, its data

The role of relationships in learning, in human development, and in moral reasoning is at the heart of the questions feminist assessment poses and the methods it chooses to use to gather data

gathering, and its analysis to have a relationship to actions we will take. Rather than an abstraction floating without any ties to the concrete, feminist assessment is action-oriented and encourages social change to be achieved as an outcome of the process.

In our study, diverse sites stressed the feminist activist principles of *collaboration and collectivity*. This emphasis can be seen in the series of potluck suppers with faculty members, students, and staff members on campuses and in the retreats and collective conversations at other sites where initial ideas were formulated and assessment strategies were planned. Also in keeping with feminist activism, the voices of the many, as opposed to the preaching of the few, are legitimated in feminist assessment. Collaboration and collectivity consider the whole—the whole learner, the whole community, the whole program—as they look to many sources for a more complete picture of what is being assessed or evaluated.

In this current investigation, the feminist belief in the *concept of creating ways to give voice to those who might otherwise not be heard* also was demonstrated by the heavy emphasis on interviews, both individual and group; classroom teacher/student verbal interactions; individual and dialogic journals; and performance assessment of the kind discovered at Lewis and Clark College, in which undergraduate students presented papers at an annual conference as a culminating activity.

♦ *Principle 7: Feminist assessment is heavily shaped by the power of feminist pedagogy.*
Feminist pedagogy is rooted in and informed by relationships. In fact, a core contribution of feminist thought is the recognition of the role of relationships in learning, in human development, and in moral reasoning. Not surprisingly, the concept of relationship is at the heart of the kinds of questions feminist assessment poses and the methods it chooses to use to gather data.

Learner outcomes cannot be separated from teacher pedagogy. Therefore, assessment instruments relying on relationships, on dialogue, and on conversation often are the overwhelming instruments of choice. Feminist assessment logically gravitates toward aural/voice assessment techniques, which value listening over looking, connection over separation, and thinking together over counting responses. This might take the form of more loosely structured focus groups, classroom observations, post-observation interviews, telephone inquiries, and open-ended surveys. Therefore, observations of classrooms become central to feminist assessment. So, too, are post-observational interviews and open-ended surveys as they ask those actually involved in the learning process to assess in some detail.

Additionally, individual journal writing, group or dialogic journal entries, and portfolios become important not only from a pedagogical perspective but also from an evaluative one. Along with feminist pedagogy, emancipatory pedagogy is frequently employed in women's studies classrooms. Both pedagogical approaches encourage all students to speak their minds in writing assignments and in class discussions. Such openness can be of use in the area of evaluation. It logically follows that students from different backgrounds be asked to reflect more broadly on the learning process itself. This kind of data, generated through student participation, can lead to the development of questions (and some answers) that one can ask about how learning should be assessed.

Feminist assessment, then, also should take into account the scholarship that has been written from a feminist pedagogical as well as from an emancipatory pedagogical perspective. It might include the works of such writers as Culley and Portuges, Gabriel and Smithson, Maher and Schniedewind, Sadker and Sadker, Tetreault, and many others.[5]

♦ *Principle 8: Feminist assessment is based on a body of feminist scholarship and feminist research methodology that is central to this interdisciplinary area.*

To be successful, feminist assessment must be compatible with feminist scholarship. It should take into consideration such concepts as maternal thinking, caring, concern and relatedness, and women's ways of knowing or connected learning.[6] These concepts can serve as the theoretical framework for feminist evaluation, a process more concerned with improvement than testing, with nurtured progression than with final judgments.

Much of feminist methodology, like feminist scholarship, finds dichotomous thinking inaccurate and therefore seeks to break down the sometimes, if not usually, artificial barriers between what frequently are presented as irreconcilable opposites. For feminist methodology, crossing paradigms and traditions does not seem to be an insurmountable obstacle. Therefore, the forms of assessment we use should be the natural outgrowth of scholarship in the field, and an emphasis on joining theory and praxis should be compatible with that body of theoretical and applied knowledge.[7]

♦ *Principle 9: Feminist assessment appreciates values.*

Feminist assessment begins with and enacts values. It does not presume to be objective in the narrow sense of the word, nor does feminist theory believe there is any such thing as a value-free "scientific" investigation. Even the ti-

Because we sought to shape assessment in a form
congruent with our scholarship and teaching, we
eventually developed an assessment that was
seamless; it is compatible with our own
theoretical framework and everyday practices

tle of this project, "The Courage to Question," flaunts its ideological prefer-
ence for and commitment to questioning. Similarly, the kinds of questions
posed at the seven campuses reveal their range of values from heightening an
awareness of diversity to empowering students to instilling a sense of social
responsibility.

The project was rooted in values from its very first gathering when each
participant was asked to create a list of her most passionate questions about
women's studies and student learning. Those questions revealed what each
person valued the most. Through extended conversations with other faculty
members, students, and staff members on each campus, the three or four
most important questions eventually became the focus of investigation.
What people measure is—or ought to be—what they value, and the way people measure it also is a choice grounded in values.

Women's studies and gender studies students are encouraged to define
their own values, to understand the relationship of values to learning, and to
analyze how values inform perspectives. In keeping with the dynamics of the
feminist classroom where such values are explored, debated, and woven in as
one of the educational goals of the women's studies class itself, feminist assessment appreciates values.

A BRIEF DISCUSSION OF THE
FEMINIST ASSESSMENT PRINCIPLES

Clearly there are several schools in the assessment movement that share
similar principles with the nine described above. In considering whether
feminist assessment was unique, we ultimately decided that what was most
unique about it was not its manifestations but its origins. That is, it is distinctive less because of where it ends up than where it begins. For participants in
our project, the definition and practice of feminist assessment is inextricably
tied to feminist theory, feminist pedagogy, and feminist methodology. Because we sought to shape assessment in a form congruent with our scholarship and teaching, we in women's studies and gender studies eventually
developed an assessment that was seamless; that is, it is compatible with our
own theoretical framework and everyday practices. In this way, learning,
teaching, and assessment are intertwined, and assessment is but a part of the
larger whole.

While its origins distinguish feminist assessment, as does the particular
configuration of the nine principles, many of the principles will be applicable
not only to women's studies and gender studies but also to burgeoning inter-

disciplinary programs as well as to traditional departments. In addition, many of the nine feminist assessment principles are applicable for universities and colleges that are attempting to recenter their curricula toward cultural pluralism as they respond to the increasing demographic diversity in the United States and the increasing consciousness of the global village we all share.

In our centeredness on students in all their instructive differences in race, class, gender, ethnicity, sexual diversity, age, and disabilities, our participatory assessment process opens up the possibility for new conversations, new insights, and new improvements in student learning. We hope, then, that feminist assessment might be a vehicle for improving student learning in women's studies and gender studies programs, while also expanding the options available in the assessment movement as a whole.

1. Sharon B. Merriam, *Case Study Research in Education: A Qualitative Approach* (San Francisco: Jossey-Bass, 1988), 169.

2. Lamar Alexander and George Bush, *America 2000: An Education Strategy* (Washington: Government Printing Office, 1991).

3. Joan Poliner Shapiro, "Participatory Evaluation: Towards a Transformation of Assessment for Women's Studies Programs and Projects," *Educational Evaluation and Policy Analysis* 10 (Fall 1988): 191–99.

4. Malcolm Parlett and Garry Dearden, *Introduction to Illuminative Evaluation: Studies in Higher Education* (Cardiff-by-Sea, Calif.: Pacific Sounding Press, 1977). See also Joan P. Shapiro and Beth Reed, "Illuminative Evaluation: Meeting the Special Needs of Feminist Projects," *Humanity and Society* 8 (1984): 432–41, as well as Joan P. Shapiro and Beth Reed, "Considerations of Ethical Issues in the Assessment of Feminist Projects: A Case Study Using Illuminative Evaluation," in *Feminist Ethics and Social Science Research*, Nebraska Feminist Collective, eds. (New York: Mellon Press, 1988), 100–18.

5. Margo Culley and Catherine Portuges, eds., *Gendered Subjects: The Dynamics of Feminist Teaching* (Boston: Routledge and Kegan Paul, 1985); Susan L. Gabriel and Isaiah Smithson, eds., *Gender in the Classroom: Power and Pedagogy* (Urbana, Ill.: University of Illinois Press, 1990); Frinde Maher and Nancy Schniedewind, eds., "Feminist Pedagogy," *Women's Studies Quarterly* 15 (1987); Myra P. and David M. Sadker, *Sex Equity Handbook for Schools* (New York: Longman, 1982); Mary Kay Thompson Tetreault, "Integrating Content About Women and Gender Into the Curriculum," in *Multicultural Education: Issues and Perspectives*, J. A. Banks and C. A. McGee Banks, eds. (Boston: Allyn and Bacon, 1987), 124–44.

6. Sara Ruddick, *Maternal Thinking: Toward a Politics of Peace* (New York: Ballantine Books, 1989); Nel Noddings, *Caring: A Feminist Approach to Ethics and Moral Education* (Berkeley, Calif.: University of California Press, 1984); Carol Gilligan, *In a Different Voice: Psychological Theory and Women's Development* (Cambridge: Harvard University Press, 1982); Carol Gilligan, Janie Victoria Ward, and Jill McLean Taylor, *Mapping the Moral Domain: A Contribution of Women's Thinking to Psychological Theory and Education* (Cambridge: Harvard University Press, 1988); Carol Gilligan, Norma P. Lyons, and Trudy J. Hammer, *Making Connections: The Rational*

Worlds of Adolescent Girls at Emma Willard School (Cambridge: Harvard University Press, 1990); Mary Field Belenky, Blythe McVicker Clinchy, Nancy Rule Goldberger, and Jill Mattuck Tarule, *Women's Ways of Knowing: The Development of Self, Voice, and Mind* (New York: Basic Books, 1986).

7. In this area of feminist methodology, there are several writers who have contributed to our understanding of the field, among them Gloria Bowles and Renate Duelli-Klein, eds., *Theories of Women's Studies* (London: Routledge & Kegen Paul, 1983); Mary Daly, *Beyond God the Father* (Boston: Beacon Press, 1973); Sandra Harding and M. Hintikka, eds., *Discovering Reality: Feminist Perspectives on Epistemology, Metaphysics, Methodology, and Philosophy of Science* (Dordrecht, Holland: D. Reidel, 1983); Patti Lather, *Getting Smart: Feminist Research and Pedagogy With/in the Postmodern* (New York: Routledge, 1991); and Liz Stanley and Sue Wise, *Breaking Out: Feminist Consciousness and Feminist Research* (London: Routledge & Kegen Paul, 1983).

CHAPTER FOUR

———————————■———————————

ASSESSMENT DESIGNS
AND THE COURAGE
TO INNOVATE

BY JILL MATTUCK TARULE AND MARY KAY THOMPSON TETREAULT

Resistance, whether psychological or political, can be viewed as obstructive or informative, as a statement of refusal or an assertion of a different view, a position, a "standpoint," an emerging theory.[1] As the "Courage to Question" project met over the three years, the forms of resistance to assessment—as a word, a set of practices, or a tool of the majority culture—flourished in our conversations. We paid attention to the resistance, naming it as a source for ideas. We understood that new insight, invention, even wisdom, often reside (albeit hidden and silent) at the core of resistance.

We talked about resistance as we expressed feelings of aversion or dislike or simple disinterest toward assessment, and together we began to narrate for ourselves a set of alternative views, attempting to imagine how the process of assessment could serve each campus and the general project goals productively. Though perhaps not consciously, the process in the twice-yearly project meetings of members of the National Assessment Team intertwined with the process at each site and even, to some extent, in the individual assessment activities. In conversation, we began to know what mattered. The learning, as Bruffee so aptly says, was not *in* the conversation, it *was* the conversation.[2]

> "Narrate" is from the Latin *narrare* (to tell) which is akin to the Latin *gnarus* ("knowing," "acquainted with," "expert in"), both derivative from the Indo-European root *gna* ("to know")....
> Narrative is, it would seem, rather an appropriate term for a reflexive activity which seeks to "know"...antecedent events and the meaning of those events....[3]

In recent years, studies and research models have turned to narrative as a way to explore events and their meaning, as a way to examine diverse "objects" of study such as individuals, classrooms, institutions, and cultures. At the heart of narrative lies conversation and language, whether in interviews, journals, focus groups, or public meetings. Talking is narrative, stories are narrative. All the meetings of the "Courage to Question" project were narrative-rich dialogues between people that shaped and defined the project. In short, they became the project. For that is the other aspect of narrative. It is

For many academics, assessment is a troublesome
issue swimming somewhere in the bywaters of
the academy's true purposes: scholarship,
teaching, maybe service

---

a way of constructing knowledge in social contexts. It assumes a relationship between people in a community.

Thus, narrative is the medium of choice for the study of relationships. The "Courage to Question" project began to define assessment as an attempt to explore relationships between people (teacher/student; teacher/teacher; student/student), between people and ideas or activities (student/class; student/women's studies programs) and between systems (course/program; program/institution). Assessment reflects the recent work on the primacy of relationships in human development and learning and a parallel focus on the importance of narrative as both epistemology and method. It can be seen as a systematic (and systemic) narrating of a story about a particular set of relationships within a given institutional context.

Understanding assessment this way rescues it from too-rapid, unconsidered conventional approaches to research, approaches shaped by the empiricist model of distance, separation, and logical-deductive proofs as the route to both interpretation and understanding. As Carolyn Matalese puts it: "The interpretive act is replacing the objective gaze."[4] Narrative as socially constructed knowing is an interpretive act. Assessment grounded in narrative is thus repositioned as a "reflexive activity that seeks to know."

CONTEXT AND BEGINNINGS

FINDING THE QUESTIONS

Assessment usually begins with some set of questions, some inquiry that promises to provide increased expertise in a given conversation or set of conversations. It is not always easy, however, to get to the questions. The questions for this project gradually developed over the first year. A set of four principles to explore (knowledge base, critical skills, feminist pedagogy, and personal growth) was transformed in these conversations.

The project began locating questions, using free writing as a technique for narrating both resistance and what people wanted to know. Each participant did a "free write" on questions of personal concern. Understanding free writes as a process for narrating one's own thinking, participants generated questions to pursue. The resulting material demonstrated that this was a narrative "way of knowing" that, although informal, securely located our work together in a conversational, narrative mode.

Three questions summarize what needed to be asked at that particular moment in the process of developing assessment designs:

▶ What do I want to know?
▶ Why do I want to know it?
▶ Who is the audience for my assessment?

We struggled to find a way to address these questions that crossed the boundary from the general to the particular, that admitted value-laden and program specific concerns. This is a critical moment in creating innovative assessment. "Passionate questions" can get fished out of the dominant discourse, whether that discourse is about how "good" assessment proceeds or about whether a marginal academic program can withstand comparison with other discipline programs and the mainstream curriculum as a whole, or about what assessment questions themselves have to be.

At best, this moment for locating questions of genuine concern allows the questioner to position herself in relationship to the process about to begin. For many academics, assessment is a troublesome issue swimming somewhere in the bywaters of the academy's true purposes: scholarship, teaching, maybe service. Recent calls for new definitions of scholarship aside, the most frequent resistance to program assessment was that it was not only an uninteresting activity but that it also was quite unrelated to the reward system of academia.[5] In fact, assessment often is as unrelated to those rewards as is participation in women's studies.

Two general purposes can be served by the "free write" approach. First, it is a chance to locate questions of genuine concern. Second, it is a way to begin a process of locating the assessment effort and design in some relationship to the dominant culture. Such a location can identify boundaries as clarity emerges about which conversations in the academy the questions will address and which it will not. The University of Colorado found that in this process their inquiry had a new purpose: "more descriptive than evaluative."[6] Previously, their women's studies program had dutifully responded to a statewide mandate for assessment with "compliance rather than enthusiasm." In contrast, their new conversations brought them to an inquiry that intrigued them because it promised a conversation about things that meant something to them.

Similarly, the University of Missouri was subject to state mandated assessment. Their faculty members viewed assessment "primarily as a weapon to be used against them." Missouri's free write helped them realize that pedagogy was at the heart of their inquiries—which, in turn, helped them to initiate this assessment design with a series of faculty development workshops.

Free writes alone were not the only question-locating activity. The

University of Colorado's conversations had begun at potluck dinners with students to discuss what they learned. Old Dominion University, Hunter College, the University of Missouri, and others organized women's studies retreats or faculty development days which became forums for a similar narrative activity. In each, people seeking to understand something about their program gathered to explore in conversation what that something was, understanding that the process of voicing and discussing what mattered would be a process of socially constructing a set of concerns to explore. In these meetings an inchoate transformation of the assessment process began, which is reflected in the very etymology of the word. Now the goal became much more to assess in the sense of sitting beside (assession) rather than the more dominant sense of the word meaning fixing or apportioning value.[7]

What began to emerge at each site were descriptions of particular inquiries within each of the institutional contexts. What the participating programs wanted to know took on a flavor of particularity and context-specific concerns. For example, Colorado found a core inquiry: "From the standpoint of student learning, what do we actually do?" With this question, they "located" their concern, detailing a particular perspective from which to view and a set of activities. Oberlin College, on the other hand, wanted to look at "some of the distinctions and tensions, as well as the commonalities, among students and faculty members of diverse racial, ethnic, class, gender, and sexual identities." They therefore emphasized "positionalities from which learning and teaching occur." Lewis and Clark College and Old Dominion University had fundamental questions about the knowledge students acquire in gender studies and women's studies classes. Each program's questions grew in a way that was appropriate and manageable, shaped by a narrative peculiar to the culture, concerns, and constraints of that institution and program while still relevant to the larger conversation of the project.

It is this final point about beginning narratives as question-locating activities that must be stressed. If narrative as a way to know and become expert is solidly grounded in relationship and in socially constructed discourse communities, it will always bear the mark of individuality and specificity and frequently, as one faculty participant observed, will seem messy—undetailed and not amenable to easy generalization.

EXPANDING THE QUESTIONS TO A DESIGN

The mess itself can seem overwhelming: too disordered, too complex, and too embedded in a dialogue among the convinced. A second set of questions can lead out of this morass, which the projects themselves turned toward as part of their conversations. Colorado's question about student experience developed in response to questions they had generated. Old Dominion, having located particular areas of learning to question, developed small discussion groups to bring greater detail to those questions. Generally, for all sites, the questions at this point were:

▶ How can we find out what we want to know?
▶ Who are our best informants?
▶ Who is the audience for our assessment?

Often shorter in time than the preceding dialogues, the conversations addressing these questions begin the process of zeroing in on significant ideas, on who can help to develop those specific ideas, and on an imagined conversation those ideas can promote. In addition, the second question prompts a specific turn to assessment methods.

By this point, the ongoing narratives had moved beyond the typical questions of research—validity, reliability, and universality—to critical moments of individuation. The programs all found their concerns turning toward their own developing narratives and toward what had emerged as meaningful for them to explore. To some extent, this left behind many of the previous concerns, especially conversations about their programs' marginality. This move helped to diminish the idea that assessment would lead toward some definitive response to the majority culture.

There are many ways to understand the nature of this critical juncture. It can be seen as what Audre Lorde so aptly describes as the fact that one can't dismantle the master's house using the master's tools.[8] Or it can be seen as a particular stage in a process of feminist phases of curriculum development, where the epistemological challenge to dominant ideologies and practices is explicit and worthy of development on its own and as a route to transforming epistemological frameworks altogether. Or it can be understood as a time when the narrative process is uniquely balanced with the process of listening, when the questions themselves essentially create their own context and other contexts grow paler, less figural, more background. Finally, it can be understood as an essential moment in which each program left behind *defining* feminist assessment and instead took up actually *doing* it. They turned their attention to creating designs that were appropriate and to understanding that, in some way, what made those designs feminist was that they were being done by feminists with processes that they identified *as* feminist.

Regardless of which analysis fits best, a general outcome from this mo-

One of the important things learned from the
project had to do with the courage to question
conventional research design and analysis
strategies

---

ment is that the concern with audience seems to abate at this point. That is, the answer to the audience question became more like "Let's wait to see what we have to say before we decide who we want to talk to." Conversation turns to narrating what is of real concern. "We welcomed the opportunity to pause and focus on student learning," explains Lewis and Clark. It seems likely that without this change in the conversation, most innovation, experimentation, or maybe any assessment dies on the way to being born, silenced by imaginary critics before any data have been collected. The audience has been considered an integral part of the conversations to this point. Now the audience must be ignored if one is successfully to get to the question—"How can we find out what we want to know?"—and create responses to that methods question in a way that honors the preceding conversations.

Thus, innovative methods do not spring full-blown from a set of goals or objectives. Achieving unique or innovative ways of inquiry requires creating conditions that support the endeavor. Notably, those conditions echo the principles detailed in Joan Poliner Shapiro's chapter, "What is Feminist Assessment?" Grounded always in narrative exploration, this approach is participatory. It redefines the relationship between the researcher and the researched. It is value-laden, relational, context-specific, collaborative, and concerned with process. Innovative methods not only emerge from the dialogue, the narrative of each program, and its concerns, they also enhance that dialogue. In so doing, they often lead to a revised relationship between not only subject and object but also process and product. The assessment designs that emerged manifested these revisions.

THE ASSESSMENT PROCESS

HOW CAN WE FIND OUT WHAT WE WANT TO KNOW?

There is an old adage floating around among certain researchers, particularly those devoted to narrative, that goes something like, "Don't collect more data than you want to analyze." One of the important things learned from the "Courage to Question" project had to do with the courage to question conventional research design and analysis strategies. Growing out of a general concern with narrative as an epistemological framework and a productive process, both the development of designs and the analyses of data took on principles of narrative-based inquiry: a concern with stories, an assumption of the relevance of experience, and a willingness or courage to examine both the nature and the outcome of conversation. In this time when case study (and portfolios as specific, individualized case studies) is beginning to be viewed as a productive line of inquiry and research, the project joined those efforts—either in fact or in spirit—with a concern for locating ways to examine what, in Patton's terrific phrase, "is actually going on."

This section explores what some of those innovative designs were and the analyses they supported. However, a word of reminder is required. Adopting any of these approaches without reference to context and without the supportive and explorative conversations that preceded them will, at best, influence any salutary outcome and, at worst, diminish the value of the approach and render the analysis irrelevant or damaging.

METHODS AND INSTRUMENTS
As the campuses turned to the question of how to find out what they wanted to know, they turned to an array of "instruments" for that purpose. With a set of defined concerns—referred to as goals or questions or areas to explore—each women's studies and gender studies program began to examine and locate effective and parsimonious ways to collect data. The questions at this point echo some of the earlier ones but now with a different end in mind:

▶ What do I want to know?
▶ Who are the best informants?
▶ How will I find out?

On the whole, the data collection instruments of the "Courage to Question" project do not, in and of themselves, represent radical departures from conventional practice; given the preceding work, however, the meaning of both their use and the processes for analysis hang close to narrative principles. New uses of standard practice can count as innovation.

Standard practice would dictate the use of designed instruments such as questionnaires and interview protocols for either individual or focus group interviews, as well as unobtrusive measures such as observation or the use of existing documents for analysis. All of these were used in the project, but the combinations of them within the particular contexts created distinct assessment designs in each case. Moreover, the usual distinctions between designed or unobtrusive measures, as well as between quantitative and qualitative analysis, diminished. Most sites did some of both, and all found unique ways to collect and analyze data. In each case, the narrative approach flourished as student experience was placed at the center of the inquiry. While other people's experience—particularly faculty members'—were examined, all seven campus-based projects focused their inquiry on some variation of

Attention to students' language and the
naturalistic narratives they produce reflects an
ongoing concern with the meaning being
constructed by students and the kind of
learning that meaning represents

---

the core question about what students themselves experienced in the women's studies and gender studies programs.

Many projects developed their own questionnaires. Wellesley, Old Dominion, and Lewis and Clark created questionnaires to explore alumnae/i's experience of the program and their learning in it. Questionnaires also were developed for students in the program, and sometimes for control groups of students not in the women's studies program, to inquire how they learned, the particular nature of the knowledge gleaned, and what kind of classroom dynamics were operating.

Old Dominion, for example, created a pre- and post-test for a group of classes to question what knowledge-based learning was occurring on particular vectors, such as the social construction of gender, interlocking oppression of women, women's varied relations to patriarchy, social construction of knowledge, or women's power and empowerment. Like many of the other campuses, Old Dominion not only pursued these questions through the tests and questionnaires but also began looking at unobtrusive measures—data generated in the paper-laden, test-laden, routine processes of the academy. In these cases, the generation of data is not a problem. It occurs in the daily processes of the classes and programs. Creating ways to access that data and analyze it is the challenge.

This was a challenge that many took on, in some cases choosing unobtrusive measures that were especially creative. At least three of the campuses examined existing processes for honoring student work and analyzed those works for varied purposes ranging from content to critical reasoning to knowledge base questions. Questions often were embedded in course exams. Colorado students were asked to compile a portfolio of their work in the women's studies program and conduct an analysis of what they had learned. Old Dominion asked a question about students' friendships, both at the beginning and end of a semester of classes. A number of programs analyzed student papers or journals to determine the nature of knowledge demonstrated. This attention to students' language and the naturalistic narratives they produce in the course of a semester or a year reflected an ongoing concern with paying attention to the meaning being constructed by students and the kind of learning that meaning represented.

Another approach to locating and listening to students' meaning emerged in focus-group interviews. At Hunter College, a graduating senior conducted these interviews with a cross-section of women's studies students and graduates as her final project. As mentioned above, a number of sites used essentially focus-group interview strategies to generate questions to pursue or to find out how students or faculty members were experiencing the program. Wellesley conducted both telephone and face-to-face interviews with students, alumnae, and faculty members to explore in greater depth what their open-ended questionnaire asked.

Observation also can be viewed as a relatively unobtrusive measure. Also involving a student as primary investigator, Colorado undertook to observe both women's studies classes and comparable classes in the humanities and social sciences. Grounded in the narrative-friendly approach of "illuminative evaluation," in which there is a process of "progressive focusing" on the questions at hand, the classroom observations included three components: content, structure, and dynamics. Hunter undertook a less formal observational approach by examining existing practices and the use of them. Looking at recently awarded student prizes, students' choice of internship sites, student fairs, and student organizations, they evaluated the extent to which their goal of achieving a multicultural emphasis in the women's studies program was apparent in these activities.

Overall, what seemed particularly significant in the data collection phase of the process was that each program found a way to collect information that was minimally disruptive and not too time consuming. Given busy schedules and the demands of teaching, this was absolutely necessary. Each program was quite capable of creating highly complex assessment programs which could easily have been accomplished had there been unlimited time and funds. What is exemplary and laudatory is that the data actually collected seemed both negligibly intrusive and unimaginably rich.

MAKING MEANING: THE PROCESS OF ANALYZING RESULTS

While most of the data collection activities were essentially narrative in practice, reliant upon conversations and writing, the narrative process for constructing meaning flourishes as the data analysis begins. At the heart of data analysis lies a process of making meaning, of looking at a set of complex or confusing materials and beginning to discern nuggets of insight, a sense of what matters and what is happening and ideas for further research.

Unless one reads the entire report of the seven individual projects, it is rather difficult to convey the richness of ideas that emerged. As attention turned to data analysis, often there was again a rich conversation to support it. Preliminary reports, themselves frequently written collaboratively, typically were taken back to a group of faculty members or faculty members and students. Such collaboration among analyzers was noted by many as an opportunity to further both professional work and personal relationships as well as to refine program designs, curriculum, or pedagogy.

In some cases, data analysis was seamless with data collection. Undertaking a fairly recent innovation in the coding of qualitative data, many did "multiple readings" of the same set of data, so that one set of materials could be viewed from a couple of perspectives.[9] Wellesley, for instance, collected quantitative data comparing women's studies and non-women's studies courses. They then went back to the student questionnaires to reinterpret the numbers on the basis of the more extended short-answer narratives students included as part of their response. Lewis and Clark gathered journals, papers, exams, and questionnaires to examine the intellectual progression through which students incorporated a set of knowledge plots in gender studies. They then reviewed those same sources to look at the pattern of responses from male students versus that of female students. Like all good conversations, multiple readings recognize that meaning is multilayered and only the opportunity to "replay" the conversation, listening for the different themes, both captures and honors the complexity.

What seems most significant in the process of data analysis is actually two-fold. First, there is a process of bringing certain questions to the fore in looking at any materials. A number of the campuses began with some quantitative analysis—often as a starting point and particularly as a way to frame comparative questions about women's studies courses or students in contrast to non-women's studies courses or students. Some developed a way to code data for particular components. For example, Lewis and Clark developed a series of coding sheets to inquire of class syllabi how much gender-based, socially constructed knowledge was integrated into the courses. Similarly, they "scored" student papers for knowledge base, as did Old Dominion with student exams and papers. But even if data analysis did not initially start with a simple or single analytic technique, all of the sites moved toward illuminating particular questions of concern—toward examining the material with some a priori questions and some that emerged as the analysis progressed.

The second aspect of this kind of analysis is that narrative inquiry again becomes both a salient and informative procedure. Just as the early conversations constructed meaning in context, so does data analysis construct meaning from the data/narratives. The process is dialectic, emergent, exploratory, and sometimes described as "soft" as opposed to "hard." By staying close to one's questions and the material, a clearer picture or fuller story begins to emerge.

RETURNING TO THE CONVERSATION

It is those compelling stories that are told in the individual reports. Each campus found it had particular things to say about the strengths and challenges in its program. For some, the data analysis moved them back into a conversation with a particular literature. Colorado's report examines the contribution of women's studies content, structure, and dynamics in the context of the current literature on the quality of undergraduate programs. Wellesley suggests how some of their findings reverberate with "different voice theory" of women's development and learning, while Old Dominion examines their students' cognitive developmental position and the impact it has on interpreting not only the student's experience but also the data they examined. In short, the interpretative act is powerfully foregrounded in all the analyses—sometimes in confident statements grounded in data, sometimes in further questions to pursue.

But the final reports are not, like women's conversational style, peppered with tag questions and open-ended, hypothesis-generating statements. Clearly the inquiry has led to significant recommendations in all cases: recommendations for further study to be sure, but also specific recommendations such as sequencing or prerequisites for particular courses of study; re-envisioning involvement of students; and pedagogical refinements to ensure more connected learning, in terms of both active involvement and personalized learning. Recommendations are made that address all levels of the academic project: teaching, curriculum, and co-curricular activities.

In addition, there is a series of outcomes which, in a more conventional approach to assessment, might be ignored. Yet we would argue they are critical to the health and well-being of the institutions, the participants, and the assessment process itself. A number of institutions observed that the mere intention of undertaking assessment and the energy put toward it spawned a renewed vitality. Student groups that had been dormant revived and began operating again. In some cases the process of identifying alumnae/i led to a revival or creation of an alumnae/i group, though the process was not always straightforward or simple (on one campus it took a year to get the registrar's office to state definitively that it had no way to access information about graduates' majors). Most notably, a number of places that did not have active conversations among faculty members found that the assessment project fostered lively and ongoing discussions; those faculty members vowed to maintain and continue both the conversation and the assessment.

In its best form, assessment contributes to the life of an academy in a

In its best form, assessment contributes to the life
of an academy in a way that promotes further
thought, interpersonal and professional
connections, and enhanced student
development opportunities

---

way that promotes further thought, interpersonal and professional connections, and enhanced student development opportunities. To begin any assessment project is to enter into a conversation about all the important issues in
education: What are we hoping students learn (goals)? How do we arrange
things so they learn that (curriculum, pedagogy, requirements)? Do we think
it is happening, and, if not, how might it happen better (evaluation)?

If the recent calls for renewed vigor and attention to teaching are to be
taken seriously, the move to assessment must support that effort. The means
of assessment will always be shaped by the ends it is intended to accomplish
or address. When it is grounded in a conversation, and when that conversation starts with having the courage to question not only what we do but also
what we think we do, it will become a rich dialogue about the nature of learning, about the nature of knowledge, and particularly about the insights that
programs struggling on the margins have to tell us about the limits of practice
in the center. As the "Courage to Question" project participants came to the
end of their reports, it was clear that they were prepared—even eager—to re-
join the conversation. The audience for their insights had become clear,
though different at each site, and without a doubt they will continue to have
rich narratives and important contributions to make in that dialogue.

---

1. See Carol Gilligan, Annie G. Rogers, and Deborah L. Tolman, *Women, Girls, and
Psychotherapy: Reframing Resistance* (New York: Haworth Press, 1991); Sandra Harding, *The
Science Question in Feminism* (Ithaca, N.Y.: Cornell University Press, 1986); Frances Maher and
Mary Kay Thompson Tetreault, *Inside Women's Classrooms: Mastery, Voice, Authority, and
Positionality* (forthcoming); Elizabeth V. Spelman, *Inessential Women: Problems of Exclusion in
Feminist Thought* (Boston: Beacon Press, 1988).
2. Kenneth A. Bruffee, "On Not Listening in Order to Hear, Collaborative Learning and the
Rewards of Classroom Research," *Journal of Basic Writing* 7 (1988): 1–12.
3. V. Turner, "Social Dramas and Stories about Them," in *On Narrative*, W. J. T. Mitchell, ed.
(Chicago: Univ. of Chicago Press, 1981), 164.
4. Carolyn Matalese, "Feminist Pedagogy and Assessment" (presentation at the American
Association for Higher Education 1992 Assessment Conference, Miami, June 1992).
5. Ernest L. Boyer, *Scholarship Reconsidered: Priorities of the Professoriat* (Princeton, N.J.: The
Carnegie Foundation for the Advancement of Teaching, 1990).
6. This and subsequent quotations describing the project come from the campus reports.
7. See the Oxford English Dictionary.
8. Audre Lorde, *Sister/Outsider* (Trumansburg, N.Y.: The Crossing Press, 1984), 112.
9. Lyn Mikel Brown, ed., *A Guide to Reading Narratives of Moral Conflict and Choice for Self and
Social Work* (Cambridge: Harvard University Graduate School of Education, 1988).

CHAPTER FIVE

■

SEASONING YOUR OWN SPAGHETTI SAUCE

AN OVERVIEW OF METHODS AND MODELS

BY CAROLYNE W. ARNOLD

There were three principal charges to the National Assessment Team (NATs). We were to introduce site participants to the wide variety of assessment methods available, both qualitative and quantitative; assist them in devising assessment strategies and procedures custom-tailored to the needs and specifications of their particular campuses; and provide practical training in how to design assessment instruments, collect and analyze data, interpret results, and report findings. Our task, then, was not to create a unified, standardized assessment plan to be adopted by all seven women's studies programs. Instead, we were to provide participants with an array of strategies they could adapt to the specific questions each different institution intended to pose about student learning. As one gourmand among us put it memorably, assessment means "seasoning your own spaghetti sauce." We assessment experts were to introduce the seasonings available in the spice cabinet.

As outside consultants, we appropriately represented a variety of areas of expertise and a range of experience using different kinds of instruments, from interviews to questionnaires; from dialogic journals to focus groups; from ethnographic observations to statistical comparisons. Two of us were trained in quantitative assessment, two had special strengths in developmental models, one had focused her research on an ethnographic model, five had used a range of qualitative approaches, and all were familiar with key concepts in women's studies. Among the six of us, we had more than a century's worth of hands-on experience in assessment and evaluation on campuses, in policy centers, or at the national level.

Throughout our training sessions, we emphasized the importance of developing an assessment plan that would be appropriate for each of the institutions and that would reveal the greatest information about the questions each women's studies program had posed about student learning in their classes. Each of us recognized that not all assessment techniques were appropriate for all things or all institutions. We also felt challenged to find a way to develop an emerging assessment methodology that would be commensurate with feminist theory, pedagogy, and practice.

Overriding all the models and methods we presented were the two familiar overarching notions of evaluation: formative evaluation and summative evaluation. Formative evaluation is oriented toward gathering data that will allow decision makers to make informed choices about improving an existing program. Ideally, formative evaluation results in clarification of goals, objectives, and program revisions during the course of the assessment that allows for mid-course corrections. There is wide latitude in selecting methodologies, types, and sources of data including study subjects and means of data gathering. The primary aim is to generate data that present comprehensive information about designated problems, issues, and questions from the perspectives of students, faculty members, alumni, administrations, and others.

Summative evaluation, by contrast, is a process by which data are gathered to determine the effectiveness and continued viability of a program. Findings and results are used to prove the value and worth of a program, to justify its need, or to make a go or no-go decision about whether to keep the program. Whichever approach, each site was encouraged to select the model that best fit its special circumstances, to define program goals in areas that affected student learning, and to derive student learning objectives based upon these goals. What follows are brief glimpses of some of the possible assessment methods we offered to participating institutions.

FEMINIST ETHNOGRAPHY

Mary Kay Thompson Tetreault, whose earlier work examined developmental phases for faculty and curriculum development, is dean of the School of Human Development and Community Service at California State University–Fullerton. In collaboration with Frances Maher, she has done extensive work in developing feminist ethnography as an assessment method.[1] Tetreault's research area has focused increasingly on direct observation of classroom dynamics and culture.

Feminist ethnography explores an approach that seeks to immerse researchers in the culture of each institution—and within that context, each classroom—to enable them to decipher meanings that participants make of events. The researchers seek continually to be conscious of the different positions and points of view presented in transcript and interview data by the study subjects—the professors, the students, and themselves. In other words, this methodology seeks to juxtapose and display the perspectives of the researchers, the informants, and the reader by putting them into explicit relationships with one another.[2]

According to the authors, in feminist ethnography sources of data may be transcripts or observations of class discussions and classrooms or interviews with teachers and students. Data are analyzed line by line, which allows interpretations of patterns of what gets said, by whom, and in what sequence statements are made. Using such a technique reveals the interactions of different student viewpoints and permits an analysis that incorporates the influence of gender, race, age, and other differentials that affect the process of knowledge construction. Transcripts show the role of the participants' "situated knowledge" or "positionality" in weaving together and balancing different versions of feminism and "partial truths."

ILLUMINATIVE AND PARTICIPATORY EVALUATION

Another of the NATs—Joan Poliner Shapiro, associate dean of the College of Education at Temple University—has researched and written about illuminative and participatory approaches to assessment.[3] In earlier writings, Shapiro focused primarily on illuminative evaluation as an approach for assessing women's studies programs and projects.[4] As Shapiro explains, illuminative evaluation is an alternative model of evaluation which was one of the first to deal with some, though not all, of the criticisms and questions raised by feminist and nontraditional educational evaluations.

The illuminative model is used as an example of a nontraditional approach to measure the success or failure of innovative projects and encompasses the phenomenological and ethnographic mode as well. Illuminative evaluation is so broad-based that it utilizes not only the techniques of participant observation, interviews, and analysis of documents in the form of a case study but also, where appropriate, incorporates questionnaires and other quantifiable instruments. The advantage of illuminative evaluation is that both qualitative and quantitative methods can be combined to "illuminate the subject."

Illuminative evaluation, as a strategy, makes no claim to perfect objectivity. The evaluation is not supposed to be value- free. Illuminative evaluation also is a form of assessment that can be called goal-free and, thus, is particularly useful for evaluating new programs when long-term effects cannot be anticipated.[5] The illuminative approach also has a number of qualities that would seemingly make it well suited for assessing women's studies programs. Before the strategy is employed, however, both its strengths and weaknesses as a methodology should be fully explored to ascertain whether or not it is appropriate for a given setting.

Like illuminative evaluation, participatory evaluation is interactive in

Participatory evaluation allows the evaluator
to be a knowledgeable insider and no longer
confines the assessor to the impartial
outsider role

---

its approach. This technique contains both qualitative and quantitative methodologies and is well suited for measurements of subtle and not-so-subtle changes. Participatory evaluation allows the evaluator to be a knowledgeable insider and no longer confines the assessor to the impartial outsider role. Many believe this type of relationship is more conducive to engendering greater trust between the evaluator and those being evaluated. It tries to avoid the subject/object split, enabling those participants whose voices may not typically be heard to speak.

Qualitative methods such as participant observation, textual analysis, and interviews with participating individuals supply the data upon which findings are based. Similarly, quantitative measures such as enrollment figures and other numerical data are accepted sources of information and are readily incorporated into the assessment process. In Shapiro's participatory approach, assessment and evaluation become interchangeable. In participatory evaluation, the focus is on the improvement of aspects of the program or project over time, as opposed to an emphasis on a final judgment. In this model, the process of the evaluation is extremely important. To put it another way, formative evaluation is stressed more than summative evaluation.

Shapiro also has written in the area of feminist pedagogy. In a paper with Carroll Smith-Rosenberg, she explores student learning in an introductory women's studies ethics course by turning to the voices of the students themselves as they speak through the pages of their journals.[6] In another paper, she uses case-study analysis as a way to enable nonfeminist and feminist students, in a women's studies classroom, to better hear and understand each other.[7] In all of her writings, feminist pedagogy and assessment tend to overlap. For Shapiro, journals and case studies not only can be used as effective pedagogical approaches; they also have the potential to be used as appropriate and meaningful techniques for the assessment of student learning.

PORTFOLIOS AND ASSESSMENT

Pat Hutchings of the American Association for Higher Education has done pioneering work in developing and promoting the portfolio as a means of collecting student work over time. She is especially adept at elaborating aspects of the model in simple, direct terms that forcefully present its strengths and weaknesses. Many questions and many uses can be derived from this file of information on student learning.

According to Hutchings, portfolio assessment is "a collection of student work done over time. Beyond that, the rule is variety—and appropriately so.

One finds portfolios used for student advising on one hand, for program evaluation on the other; some portfolios include only written work, others a broader array of 'products'. Some are kept by students, some by department advisors, some by offices of assessment...."[8]

Distinctive features of portfolio assessment as listed in Hutching's article are as follows:

► Unlike many methods, portfolios tell you not only where the students end up but also how they got there.

► Portfolios put explicit emphasis on human judgment and meaning-making.

► Because they prompt (even demand) conversation, portfolios lend themselves to use.

► Portfolios are less subject to misuse than apparently simpler, single-score methods.

► Most importantly, portfolios can be educational for students.

The variety rule extends to methods of data collection as well. For example, a portfolio may include course assignments, research papers, an audiotape of a presentation, materials from a group project, and other types of work. Portfolios reveal not only outcomes—that is, what students know and can do at the end of their studies—but they get "behind outcomes." As Hutchings describes it, "They reveal learning over time and are participatory in nature. They invite conversation and debate between, for instance, the student, the department advisor, a faculty member from a support area, the director of student services, and perhaps others from external audiences." On the other hand, the disadvantages are that "they're bulky, time consuming, difficult to make sense of, maybe not what the legislature had in mind, and they are in an early, unproven stage of development."[9]

COLLABORATIVE LEARNING
AND WOMEN'S WAYS OF KNOWING

Jill Mattuck Tarule, dean of the College of Education and Social Services at the University of Vermont and one of the authors of *Women's Ways of Knowing*, encouraged participants to use collaborative learning models in their final designs. Collaborative learning shares a number of traits with women's studies. Both are learner-focused and process-focused. They each see the learner as constructing the meaning and learning as embedded in context. Both also see negotiating power lines as a fundamental task. While collaborative learning does not necessarily involve a concept of positionality, it

Separate knowing, more typically associated
with men, seeks to construct truth—to
prove, disprove, and convince. Connected
knowing, more typical of women, seeks to
construct meaning, to understand and be
understood

---

challenges students to work together in small groups, examining a particular perspective or creating a salient critique. Women's studies argues strongly that knowledge is situated—made partial because of the position of the knower to the known, especially as that is affected by race, class, gender, sexuality, and other markers. Research on cooperative and collaborative learning groups suggests that students, as they struggle to construct knowledge together, become conscious of their distinct differences rooted in their own experiences. Collaborative learning reflects an intentionality about offering a social critique that also distinguishes women's studies.

Tarule also advocated tapping as assessment resources common classroom practices that are especially rich in revealing how learning occurs over time. Among her suggestions were the dialogic journal, periodic free-writes, student journals, and student self-assessments. The dialogic journal is kept in the classroom and is designed to capture a communal record of the learning process in the class over the semester. Periodic free-writes, like the dialogic journal, might already be a regular part of a course and yet also become data read later for assessment purposes. Student journals are a variation of the two writing techniques. Some are structured with a very definite set of questions to answer; others are more free-flowing and spontaneous.

Finally, one might incorporate self-assessments into the fabric of a given course with an eye to using it later to answer some questions about course content, student learning, or class dynamics. Students can be asked early on to do a free-write on why they took the course or what key questions they hope the course will answer. In the middle of the course, students can be asked to write on what they are thinking about the course at that point. Finally, they can do a self-assessment at the end. Another variation of the self-assessment is to design it as a progress report in which the students write a letter to the professor every two weeks which the professor answers. In a course at Wellesley College, students wrote letters about why they took a specific course and then mailed them to their parents. Ultimately, all these sources of data can be examined through many different lenses. Such a data base could even become part of a longitudinal study of student learning.

Offering women's studies faculty members another lens through which to consider how students learn, Tarule presented the main contrasts between separate and connected knowing as they emerged in *Women's Ways of Knowing.*[10] Separate knowing, more typically associated with men and more valued as a way of knowing in the traditional academy, seeks to construct truth—to prove, disprove, and convince. Connected knowing, which emerged from the authors' research as more typical of women, seeks to construct meaning, to understand and be understood. While separate knowing is adversarial, connected knowing is collaborative. Where the discourse of separate knowing is logical and abstract, that of connective knowing is narrative and contextual. Instead of detachment and distance in relation to the known, the connected knower seeks attachment and closeness. While feelings are seen to cloud thought for the separate knower, feelings illuminate it for the connected knower. Objectivity for the former is achieved by adhering to impersonal and universal standards; objectivity for the latter is achieved by adopting the other's perspective. While the separate knower is narrowing and discriminating, the connected knower is expansive and inclusive. For the separate knower, there is the risk of alienation and absence of care. For the connected knower, there is the risk of loss of identity and autonomy.[11]

Tarule emphasized that separate and connected knowing are gender-related, not gender-specific. She urged faculty members to narrate with students how they do or do not go back and forth between the two ways of knowing and under what circumstances and in what contexts they choose one approach over the other. By being involved in the students' narratives of their learning processes, one can hold the complexity in tension.

CREATING PROGRAM GOALS
AND LEARNING OBJECTIVES

In discussing the relation between goals and measures, Mary Kay Thompson Tetreault posed two questions: How do we begin to conceptualize about what we want to know? What are the things that shape what we want to know? Tetreault thinks it is valuable to probe our own personal histories as students and as teachers to trigger our thinking. What do we care passionately about? How were we silenced? What is the relation of our own history to that of the new generations of students? She also urged women's studies faculty members to look at their program goals and imagine what their students might say. How would the collection of data change? Are the questions the right questions for students? As they formulated goals, Tetreault reminded faculty members to be conscious of their own partial perspectives and ways to enhance that partiality with a variety of other people's perspectives.

As a specialist in the field of public health and as the assessment expert who relied in my research predominantly on quantitative methods, I was to function as a resource for those who were interested in developing more statistically-oriented instruments. One of the most prevalent misconceptions is

One of the most prevalent misconceptions is that
quantitative and qualitative evaluation are
necessarily in opposition; the two used together
can reveal different and illuminating information
about a given subject

---

that quantitative and qualitative evaluation are necessarily in opposition.
Because they can actually complement one another, the two used together
can reveal different and illuminating information about a given subject.
Most campuses in our project ended up using a combination of quantitative
and qualitative methods to assess student learning. The method finally cho-
sen depends on the question, issue, or problem you want to examine or solve.

In creating instruments used in quantitative analysis, it is important to
use language that can be translated into measurable outcomes. "Recognize,"
"describe," and "identify," for instance, are easier to measure than "appreciate," "engage," or "foster." Similarly, skills or learning behaviors you can see
and observe lend themselves more easily to having a numerical value at-
tached to them. In the preliminary goal statements each women's studies
program prepared, a number of problems stood out which are common when
first setting up an assessment plan:

▶ Participants were unclear about the conceptual distinction between goals
and objectives. They did not make the distinction of separating the concept (the goal) from the measurement of it (the objective).

▶ There often was a blurring of program/department/ institutional goals,
faculty/instructional objectives, and student learning objectives.

▶ The language used to formulate and describe program goals did not convey the appropriate meaning of the concept (direction, aspiration, expectations, ideals, and purposes of the programs).

▶ The language used to define student learning objectives was vague or am-
biguous. Learning objectives did not identify and specify measurable end-
products—that is, "outcomes."

To help programs avoid such conundrums, I sought to train participants
in five areas:

▶ how to distinguish between program goals and student learning objectives
▶ how to conceptualize, formulate, and state goals in appropriate language
▶ how to derive student learning objectives from program goals
▶ how to translate student learning objectives into outcomes
▶ how to translate outcomes into measurable (quantifiable) indicators of
student learning.

A program goal actually is no more than a generalized statement expressing a
program's expectations, a "timeless statement of aspiration." Program goals
should be stated in terms that are clear, specific, and measurable. They also
should express consensus about what the program aims to do.

Developing program goals is useful in any assessment project because they establish the program's rationale, framework, and parameters. They also serve as the philosophical justification for the program's existence. Many in our project found that program goals gave their program focus and direction. For assessment purposes, they also serve as a monitor to gauge a program's accomplishments. In the case of the "Courage to Question" project, we used the creation of program goals as a way to determine specific areas in women's studies programs that involved the knowledge base, critical skills, personal growth, and pedagogy. In doing so, program goals ultimately can reflect the educational needs of both students and the institution. They also permit a program to focus on what students should know and be able to do.

As an assessment project on student learning takes shape, it also is important to define learning objectives clearly. Such objectives describe an outcome (intellectual or personal change) that students should be able to demonstrate or achieve as the result of an instructional activity or a formal or informal learning experience. These outcomes are observable and measurable. Learning objectives are useful because they specify what students are expected to be able to *do* expressly as a result of instruction. Ultimately, they form the basis for evaluating the success or failure of instructional efforts. They also supply valuable feedback to both the students and the instructor. In addition, they serve as a vehicle for developing program goals, curriculum design, teaching plans, instructional activities, and assessment activities. Because they summarize the intended outcomes of the course, they can communicate to colleagues and others the intent of a course clearly and succinctly.

It is critical that women's studies programs define their program goals and thus their direction and spend time thinking about exactly what and how they want students to learn. By formulating program goals and articulating learning objectives in terms of demonstrable, measurable outcomes, faculty members can measure the success or failure of their instructional efforts.

CONCLUSION

As my colleague Joan Shapiro describes it, assessment is really just paying attention, listening, but it is also interactive and ongoing. There is no shortage of choices among assessment instruments available to help do just that. Two factors, however, are especially important to consider in designing an assessment plan: choosing multiple and appropriate measures that will produce the information you need to know and choosing methods that complement the theoretical underpinning of the academic discipline or issue you are investigating.

Drawing on a common procedure for planning qualitative assessment

Using unobtrusive and integrated measures that
are integral to the work you are doing is always
preferable to a bulky, complicated, often
expensive external measurement

designs, Tarule described a matrix that all but one of the seven participating programs adopted in creating their final assessment design. The matrix allows one to assess a particular class or an entire project. One dimension has a set of intentions or goals horizontally across the top. Listed vertically down the side are the methods or sources relied upon to discover information about the goals across the top. (See page 102.) The matrix invites multiplicity, giving several perspectives from which to view a subject area—echoing Shapiro's notion of the importance of triangulation. It also invites the use of information already embedded in what we do. Using unobtrusive and integrated measures that are integral to the work you are doing is always preferable to a bulky, complicated, often expensive external measurement.

A chemist once said that being a good chemist is like being a good cook: You need to know what you want to do, what materials you will need, and how to mix them properly. Assessment shares that culinary analogy. The National Assessment Team for "The Courage to Question" offered an array of spices for faculty members to choose from as they were posing questions about student learning in women's studies classes. Ultimately, the campuses themselves seasoned the meal according to their own tastes.

SAMPLE PRE-ASSESSMENT QUESTIONS TO POSE

ESTABLISHING CONTEXT

A. Context of the institutional environment:
Persons, Groups, and Institutions Affected and Involved
▶ Who will be involved in the planning, implementation of the assessment? Students, WS faculty members, other faculty members, colleagues, administrators, alumni, employers, professional associations, regents, trustees, government officials, politicians?
▶ Who will be the subject(s) of the assessment?
▶ Who will see the results of the measurement?
▶ Who will be affected by the results of the assessment?
▶ How will the results affect the various constituencies?

Type and Process of Assessment
▶ Did the request for assessment originate internally or from the outside?
▶ Is this a "one-time-only" assessment or is it part of an established procedure?
▶ Do you need to obtain standardized results?

▶ Do you have special resources available to assist in the planning, development, conduct, analysis of the assessment?
▶ What is the institutional attitude/climate regarding the WS program: supportive, apathetic, hostile?
▶ How do these responses to women's studies manifest themselves?
▶ Are there any potential or anticipated problems, negative consequences, pitfalls to avoid from the assessment itself or from its result?
▶ Is it important to ensure the anonymity, confidentiality, or security of the subjects, process, or results of the assessment?

B. Context of the instructional setting:
Size
▶ How many students will take the course?
▶ Will students be grouped or sectioned in some way?
▶ If so, by what criteria?
▶ What is the estimated total yearly enrollment for the course?
▶ Is there a limit on class size?
▶ If so, who sets the limit?
▶ Is there a waiting list to take the course?
▶ Who sets the criteria that determine what students will be admitted?

Environment
▶ In what type of institution will the course be taught?
▶ What is the size of the institution?
▶ Where is the institution located?
▶ In what type of location will classes be held?
▶ What type of classroom facilities are available?

Time
▶ Which period of calendar time will the course cover?
▶ How much total time is available for class sessions?
▶ How long are single class sessions?
▶ How many class sessions are there?
▶ How often do class sessions meet?
▶ Is there opportunity to hold extra class sessions, formal or informal?
▶ How much out-of-class work can be expected of the student?
▶ What are the other concurrent time demands of students? (other courses, work, families, etc.)

▶ What is the assignment and exam schedule of the course? other courses?
▶ What time of day/evening will class sessions be held?
▶ How much time is available for office hours, advising, tutoring?

Resources
▶ How much time is available for new course development? Is there an incentive?
▶ How much time is available for the development of materials prior to or during the implementation of new courses?
▶ How much time is available for course preparation?
▶ How much money and other resources are available for material developments, guest lectures, etc.?
▶ What information sources or references are available? In what form? Where are they located?
▶ What human resources may be drawn upon and to what extent?
▶ What types of supplies and equipment are available? How accessible are they?
▶ Who will teach the course?

Precedents
▶ Are there any precedents or conventions to which the instructor must adhere (grading system, pass/fail system, competency-based system, team teaching approaches, method of student selection to take course, etc.)?

C. Students as context:
Demographics
▶ What is the average age, age range of the student body, WS program, class?
▶ What races, ethnicities, intra-ethnicities, nationalities, languages?
▶ What is the sex representation?
▶ What is the economic, social, class representation of the student body, WS program, class?
▶ What is the mix of political and ideological beliefs?
▶ Is there a prevailing value system?
▶ What is the marital status representation?
▶ Do students typically have children? What are the ages of their children?
▶ Where do students typically reside—city, suburb, on campus, off campus?

▶ Are students typically employed—full-time, part-time, on campus, off campus, work study?
▶ What is the mix of types of jobs students hold?
▶ Are the students distinguished by any special physical handicaps or assets involving health, endurance, mobility, agility, vision, hearing, etc.?

Entry Level
▶ What is the general educational level of the student body, WS program, class? Immediately out of high school, transfers from community colleges, adult returners?
▶ What is the general ability level (aptitude) of the students, e.g. advanced placement, honors program, remedial, etc.?
▶ What preparation do students have in the course subject content?
▶ Have students taken WS courses before?

Background, Prerequisites, Motivations
▶ Is there anything special about the racial, ethnic, age, sex, social, cultural, economic, political background, level of educational attainment, places of residence of the student body, WS program, class?
▶ Do students tend to have serious biases or prejudices regarding the subject matter, instructor, teaching methods, etc.?
▶ What background characteristics do students have in common?
▶ Why are students taking the course?
▶ Is it required or an elective?
▶ What do students expect to get out of the course?
▶ How would you describe the level of motivation, interest?
▶ What types of rewards—immediate or long range—do students expect to gain from taking the course?
▶ What types of roles—personal and professional—are students likely to assume upon graduation? Will they take more courses, begin a family, or do both? What is the percentage of students who will assume these roles and at what stage in their lives?
▶ Under what circumstances (family life, personal life, career life) will students likely use what they will learn in the course?

1. Frances Maher's and Mary Kay Thompson Tetreault's paper, "Doing Feminist Ethnography: Lessons from Feminist Classrooms," in *The International Journal of Qualitative Studies in Education* 6 (January 1993). Their article addresses methodological issues faced in ethnographic studies of feminist teachers in different types of colleges and institutional settings.

2. Maher and Tetreault, 1990.

3. Shapiro's article—"Participatory Evaluation: Towards a Transformative of Assessment of Women's Studies Programs and Projects," *Educational Evaluation and Policy Analysis* 10 (Fall 1988): 191–99—is a thorough discussion of the evolution of these two models and their usefulness in assessing women's studies programs.

4. Shapiro, Secor, and Butchart, 1983; Shapiro and Reed, 1984; Shapiro and Reed, 1988.

5. Shapiro, 1988.

6. Shapiro and Smith-Rosenberg, 1989.

7. Shapiro, 1990.

8. Pat Hutchings,"Learning Over Time: Portfolio Assessment," *AAHE Bulletin* 42 (April 1990).

9. Ibid.

10. Mary Field Belenky, Blythe McVicker Clinchy, Nancy Rule Goldberger, and Jill Mattuck Tarule, *Women's Ways of Knowing: The Development of Self, Voice, and Mind* (New York: Basic Books, 1986).

11. Based on Belenky, Clinchy, Goldberger, and Tarule, *Women's Ways of Knowing*, 1986; and Peter Elbow, *Writing Without Teachers* (New York: Cambridge University Press, 1973). (With thanks to Hilarie Davis for her suggestions.)

PART THREE

PRACTICAL
ASSESSMENT
RESOURCES

CHAPTER SIX

■

VOICES FROM THE CAMPUSES

BY SUZANNE HYERS

IN THE BEGINNING

When Caryn McTighe Musil first telephoned to invite programs to participate in "The Courage to Question," their initial responses were much the
same as Caryn's was to the FIPSE program officer: "You're asking us to do
what?" After that, however, the responses varied. Some viewed the project
as "timely." Lewis and Clark College "welcomed the opportunity to pause
and focus on student learning." Some, such as Old Dominion University,
viewed the project with excitement, a challenge for their program that had
broad participation and support: "From the beginning, assessment of the
Women's Studies Program...was a collaborative and hands-on learning project."

Other responses were not so positive. At the University of Missouri, for
example, "faculty members had negative feelings about assessment," in part
because of their experience with state-mandated assessment that created
competition among Missouri colleges and universities: "At this institution
...assessment was politicized in such a way that many faculty members saw
[it] primarily as a weapon to be used against them." Faculty members at the
University of Colorado also had their perceptions shaded by a state-mandated program. In Colorado, they "regarded assessment as one more bureaucrat-
ic requirement for evaluation that impinged on [their] time."

A SECOND LOOK...

"The Courage to Question," however, provided a very different framework
for program evaluation. In response to the National Assessment Team's en-
couragement "to take a more comprehensive look at assessment, its purposes,
and its possibilities for self-reflection," the University of Colorado, for example, experienced a significant change, moving from state-mandated procedures to those of feminist assessment. For them, the change meant "the
setting for our process was supportive and intellectually exciting. The audience for our reports was not a state bureaucrat but other women's studies programs and educators interested in assessment."

For the University of Missouri, "The Courage to Question" provided
an alternative to the state's "rigid, quantitative, 'value-added' approach."

The first item on the 'assessment agenda' should be to determine what *your* program needs to know. Assessment is not a true/false test. It is a series of open-ended questions

---

Although the project coincided with a difficult time of transition and rearticulation of program goals at Missouri, faculty members were clear on one thing: They had a "real passion for teaching and a long-term commitment [to] exploring feminist pedagogy." Missouri followed the National Assessment Team's recommendation to listen to such strong statements: "Rather than developing a plan that would be imposed on the faculty members...we worked toward a model of assessment grounded in the activities faculty members were already carrying out in their classes.... We talked in terms of 'faculty development' instead of 'assessment', believing that a good assessment project would, in fact, contribute to better teaching." Missouri was able to pursue this project in the midst of such difficulty because the assessment goals were parallel to individual and programmatic goals.

Ironically, the resistance of faculty members to assessment was similar to the resistance of some students to material presented in women's studies classes. However, more information—as well as time, reflection, and experience—resulted in a greater understanding and general acceptance of the process of assessment—if not the word itself. ("Assessment" continues to have as problematic a reputation as the word "feminist": Many who come to believe in its principles continue to reject the language.)

The overall approach of the campuses to this project was a familiar one for women's studies programs: make one task simultaneously tackle three situations. As described in the introduction to *The Courage to Question*:

> With long experience administering programs without sufficient support, the women's studies faculty members and administrators in the project drew on that history to create assessment instruments that were embedded in what they already do; weave data analysis into student research projects; create methods that could also have a life beyond the grant such as alumnae/i questionnaires and interviews; and make use of the project to further women's studies programmatic goals....

Consequently, not only did the project accomplish its goals through creative structuring, but *after* the project the layers of meaning understood through assessment became woven into the fabric of the programs themselves. As they continue to assign research projects and administer questionnaires and course evaluations, they will evaluate them with the knowledge gained through "The Courage to Question."

WHERE TO START
"Begin with what you do already"

In every case each institution started by defining its program's goals and objectives. The University of Missouri, as noted, began the project with a simple yet strong acknowledgment of the faculty's passion for teaching. Old Dominion University had two basic reasons for participation: They wanted to find out "just what we were teaching our students and what they were learning"; and they "wanted to create stronger connections" among members of their Women's Studies Advisory Council. Wellesley College—the only women's college among the seven participating institutions—asked "what makes women's studies at a women's liberal arts college different?"

The first item on the "assessment agenda," then, should be to determine what *your* program needs to know. Assessment is not a true/false test. It is a series of open-ended questions.

"The best we can hope for is to ask better questions:
What matters in women's studies? What do we care about?"

WHAT WORKED AND WHAT DID NOT

HUNTER COLLEGE
"Assessment is not final but ongoing."

Hunter College used course syllabi, exams, paper assignments, informal classroom writings, and a survey of introductory women's studies classes with open-ended questions that explored the value of the course overall: "If you had to describe this course to a friend, what three adjectives would you use?" "Was there a balance between the survey-scope of the course and some more in-depth investigation? Please explain." The questions explored whether a sense of community was built in the classroom and whether the course met student expectations. They compared women's studies to other introductory courses. (See page 95.) Hunter believes all methods gave them invaluable material.

Hunter also investigated how effectively the program accomplished its complex goal of multiculturalism by focusing on three areas: curriculum, scholarship, and "collective conversations" with students, which were organized by a women's studies student. The voices of these students are at the center of Hunter's report, creating a particularly strong portrait not only of the program itself but also of the diversity, passion, and spirit of its students. As noted in Hunter's report, "Students valued being consulted regarding the

Assessment has lost its negative overtones of
coercion from outside forces

---

assessment project. It became a concrete way of enacting the empowerment
and cultural thinking the project itself hoped to investigate."

The project also revised faculty members' attitudes toward assessment:
"For a group of faculty, assessment has lost its negative overtones of coercion
from outside forces." Hunter also used the project to place the women's studies program at the center of institutional discussions, such as the college's
emphasis on reaching students with nontraditional backgrounds. Through
this project, Hunter created a core advocacy group for assessment which has
had "an impact university-wide in terms of Freshman Year Initiative, work
done on Undergraduate Course of Study Committee, the Committee on
Remediation, the Provost's Advisory Committee on Remedial and
Developmental Programs, and within the Faculty Delegate Assembly and
University Faculty Senate." The women's studies program is playing a role in
other campus discussions as well. "The project has focused our attention on
the relationship between women's studies and the liberal arts curriculum…
at Hunter College…there is an ongoing debate about whether to include a
pluralism and diversity requirement in basic education requirement."

UNIVERSITY OF COLORADO
"What are the passionate questions for students?"

The University of Colorado initially planned to use its participation in "The
Courage to Question" to revise previously established state-mandated assessment procedures. The year immediately preceding the FIPSE project, Colorado had complied with the state-mandated assessment program by selecting
"one knowledge goal and two skills goals to assess," using a required feminist
theory course as the source of information. The investigation went according
to plan, but "the outcome…was not especially illuminating." As a result,
Colorado was especially poised to use our assessment project as a means of re-
evaluating its assessment process.

> We were dissatisfied with the process we had developed for sever-
> al reasons. First, the state mandate created an atmosphere that
> encouraged compliance rather than enthusiasm. Our selection of
> knowledge and skills goals as well as the methods of assessment
> emerged from a desire for efficiency…. [O]ur goals and the pro-
> cess of assessing them looked very much like standard academic
> fare: one couldn't tell much difference between the women's
> studies assessment plan and those of traditional arts and sciences
> disciplines. We were resigned to the process; we didn't "own" it;

and we didn't learn much about ourselves as teachers and learners.... We had selected particular goals not simply because they might be important, but also because they were convenient....

According to its report, Colorado then "stopped asking, 'what do we want to accomplish?' and began to ask 'From the perspective of student learning, what are we actually doing?'" Faculty members went to the students directly, as other campuses did, through a series of informal meetings such as potluck dinners to seek their opinions. Following those discussions, they came up with three categories for investigation—course content, course structure, and classroom dynamics—and were interested in two questions: "(1) Were all three of these categories equally important in fostering active learning or was one component more important than the others? and (2) Was the active learning experience that our students identified with their women's studies courses unique, or could it be found in other classes?" Using illuminative evaluation for its investigation, Colorado administered questionnaires, analyzed syllabi, and chronicled classroom observations.

According to Colorado's report, "Our experience with 'The Courage to Question' has led us to abandon our previous approach and to adopt a portfolio method. Our approach rejects a method whereby faculty alone measure student learning and proceeds from the assumption of an equal partnership between students and faculty in assessing student learning."

OLD DOMINION UNIVERSITY (ODU)
"Focus on improving rather than proving."
Refusing to be limited to the four areas suggested by the project (knowledge base, learning skills, feminist pedagogy, and personal growth), ODU established a fifth area to assess—the impact of women's studies on faculty members. ODU also examined the role of students' friendships in their investigation of personal growth. Project members created specific subcommittees to examine these five areas, these subcommittees worked well and resulted in "lively conversations and debate."

In its investigations of the knowledge base, ODU attempted to identify the five main concepts instructors sought to convey to students. The method selected was a pre- and post-test administered at the beginning and end of the semester. The tests were used in more than a dozen classes over two semesters. More than six hundred students were given the pre-test; more than five hundred took the post-test. In spite of the amount of information received from the tests, they were not considered a successful assessment method:

'Closer analysis of a few pieces of good data is
more useful than a large amount of less
bounteous data'

> While these tests were the most efficient way to take a reading of
> students' awareness of some key points for each course, they were
> not a refined instrument in ascertaining what students under-
> stood. It was not always easy to distinguish between wrong an-
> swers based on students' lack of knowledge and those that were a
> function of imprecise or confusing questions.... *Much more time*
> *consuming, but more useful, was the analysis of final exams for a few*
> *courses. In retrospect, this may have been the single most valuable in-*
> *strument for knowledge base objectives.* (Italics added.)

ODU also was disappointed in the information resulting from a series of
interviews with graduating minors and alumnae who were asked to identify
"the three most important concepts that they had learned in women's studies
courses." Project participants felt these interviews resulted in "somewhat
general answers which were only moderately instructive." In addition, the
alumnae questionnaire required a considerable commitment of time to complete, which they believe was a key factor in the low return rate. According
to Anita Clair Fellman, one of the authors of ODU's report, "Closer analysis
of a few pieces of good data is more useful than a large amount of less bounteous data." More successful for ODU were investigations regarding students'
friendships and the impact of women's studies on faculty members. Again, for
the friendship investigation ODU used questionnaires administered at the beginning and end of semesters: "Does the instructor recommend or require
group discussion or group projects? Currently how many students in class are
friends? How did being in class together change [if it did] your relationship
with this person?" These questions also appeared on the minors' exit interviews and on the alumnae questionnaire, all of which provided ODU with information about students' friendships. (See page 91.)

To assess the impact of women's studies on faculty members, ODU faculty members interviewed each other—which not only generated new data but
also encouraged both internal and external dialogues among faculty members
about the influence of women's studies: "This was the first time we had faced
one another and asked, 'What are our goals?'"

ODU had a distinctly positive experience throughout this assessment
project. They had a large number of faculty members and students (more
than two dozen) who were involved in the project from the early discussions
of assessment to the design to final interpretation of the results. According to
project participants, "While inclusiveness can be cumbersome, its virtues are
the richness of diverse opinions and perspectives and the commitment of the

participants." The conclusion to ODU's report notes the impact the project had on the program overall:

> [F]or the first time we have on paper a comprehensive and clear statement about what we are doing in women's studies, a description of our women's studies program goals that we can share with others interested in developing women's studies courses in their departments. It was a validating and reassuring experience to discover that each of us does have a clear picture of what she is trying to communicate to students and that, when put together, these individual views reveal a shared vision of what the Women's Studies Program is about. We have found words to describe what we are trying to do in our classroom, and we have discovered in one another resources, knowledge, and skills that previously we may have overlooked.

OBERLIN COLLEGE

> *"Consider assessment as a movie—not a snapshot—with different angles, different cameras, and reviewed over time."*

Participants at Oberlin College designed a series of self-statements given to students in more than fifteen courses. Through these self-statements, which were administered three times during one semester, Oberlin was able to measure (and note changes in) students' perspectives over a period of time. For example, one question asked (somewhat differently) throughout the semester was: "Do you expect this class to address questions of race?" (asked at the beginning of the semester); "Does this class address questions of race? How?" (asked at mid-semester); and "Has this class addressed questions of race? How?" (asked at the end of the semester).

In addition to the self-statements, Oberlin used interviews with women's studies majors organized by other women's studies majors; faculty and alumnae questionnaires; and a series of student interviews conducted by a women's studies student. Like Hunter, Oberlin emphasized multicultural learning:

> The shape of the assessment plan...reflect[s] the growing national debate about multiculturalism and the questions asked about women's studies programs in terms of this debate: What fosters student learning and self-empowerment? How can courses encourage a relational understanding of gender, race, class, and sexuality? Does feminist pedagogy differ from other types? How do women's studies courses affect students' lives and life choices?

Oberlin forwarded questionnaires to faculty members campus-wide to ascertain the program's acceptance. Although results were generally supportive, the questionnaire did prompt the most critical responses heard throughout the project—most often from professors who had never taught a women's studies course. Those comments ranged from describing women's studies as "one big counseling session" to saying the program has "politicized and ideologized students instead of promoting objectivity in education...." Questions asked of Oberlin faculty members included: "What significant learning experiences do you think women's studies courses offer students?"; "Do you believe that women's studies courses differ in pedagogy from non-women's studies courses?"; and "Do you ever approach your subject with an integrative analysis of gender, race, class, and sexuality?" (See page 97.)

While Oberlin's report does not evaluate specifically the methods used, faculty members have incorporated assessment into their internal examination of the women's studies program and consider the process an ongoing one. They do, however, acknowledge that "assessment doesn't occur in a politically neutral space."

LEWIS AND CLARK COLLEGE
"Use multiple methods and sources of information."
Lewis and Clark College designed an ambitious assessment plan for its gender studies program that relied on three principal data collections: questionnaires, students' papers and projects, and selected course syllabi. However, the project team also drew upon data available from their annual four-day Gender Symposium papers and projects, computer conversations, students' journals and diaries, students' honors projects, practica reports, and other previously collected material. Faculty members' engagement in assessing student learning was nourished by the overall institutional climate, which invests significantly in faculty development and places a high priority on maintaining a quality, student-centered undergraduate education. The fact that Lewis and Clark honors such investigations of the curriculum, campus climate, teaching, and student learning was an important factor in the project's success.

Lewis and Clark wanted to answer three questions: How effectively do students learn and apply gender analysis? What impact has gender studies had on the classroom and institutional climate? What impact has gender studies had on the personal growth of students and alumnae? As its central organizing group, they relied on a collaborative team that included one student, one staff member, and two faculty members. Coupled with extensive campus consultation with faculty members, students, staff members, and alumnae/i, the four worked together to oversee the data collection, analyze it, and write the final report. Like Old Dominion University, they found multiple perspectives and mutually supportive collaboration enhanced their work.

A questionnaire was sent to students, faculty members, and alumnae. (See page 85.) It eventually provided both quantitative and qualitative data—a combination that Wellesley College points out is especially illuminating, since numbers alone do not reveal the full meaning of a particular response. The student questionnaire was sent to a random sampling stratified by distribution of majors, while the faculty questionnaire was sent to all faculty members teaching undergraduates. The alumnae/i questionnaire was sent to all alumnae/i who had participated in Lewis and Clark's Gender Symposium during the previous five years. The return rates of 48 percent, 46 percent, and 48 percent, respectively, were unusually high.

Self-reporting in the questionnaires could be verified by the next major data collection: student papers and projects. In order to determine how well students were able to use gender analysis in their courses, the gender studies program developed a list of eight basic concepts—referred to as knowledge plots—which became the basis of the score sheet used to do a content analysis of papers and projects. (See page 89.) Faculty members then collected papers and projects from selected gender studies courses and compared them with a similar set of materials from core curriculum courses, in both cases using longitudinal materials such as student journals or final portfolios where possible. These proved especially illuminating in recording the process of students' intellectual development. The student work was scored independently by two readers; if there was disagreement, a third reader was brought in.

For the third of the major sources of data collections, Lewis and Clark relied on syllabi from discipline-based, non-gender studies courses to determine how much gender integration had been incorporated into classes outside the gender studies program. The comparative syllabi also allowed project participants to examine what kinds of subject areas were being covered only through gender studies. The initial student questionnaires once again generated baseline information for further inquiry. In this case, students collectively named more than one hundred courses that they claimed incorporated gender perspectives. Trimming the list to what was a more manageable number, faculty members in the gender studies program selected twenty courses, divided proportionately among the three divisions of the College of Arts and

Sciences and between male and female professors. A score sheet was created to measure content based on Mary Kay Thompson Tetreault's "feminist phase theory," again scored independently.

Lewis and Clark's assessment plan was labor intensive. Halfway through the project, participants felt overwhelmed by the mountains of data they had collected. Ultimately, however, they chose to use only material that illuminated their three basic questions, knowing they could return at another time to pose additional questions. They were sustained through the process by the belief that their research would be valued on their campus, by the mutually supportive working team they had established, and by the rich information they knew would shape their program's future. Like many of the participating campuses, they developed documents from their research that they used internally in various forms for various audiences. It allowed the work to be applied both nationally and locally to improve undergraduate education.

UNIVERSITY OF MISSOURI
"Pick a plan you can do."

The University of Missouri had a relatively difficult time in the preliminary stages of the project. Not only did faculty members have negative feelings toward assessment because of past experiences with state-mandated assessment, but there also was a lack of cohesiveness within the women's studies program due to significant staffing and administrative transitions. If defining one's goals is the first step, Missouri had difficulty from the beginning. Many women's studies programs are experiencing similar situations:

> We were discovering that goals and processes clearly articulated
> in the early eighties no longer had consensus backing from mem-
> bers of the committee. The second half of the 1980s had been a
> period of consolidation and institutionalization for the program.
> Departments began hiring faculty with expertise in women's
> studies, greatly expanding the course offerings as well as partici-
> pation in the program. Yet these women had not been involved
> in the development of the program and did not necessarily share
> the perspectives of those who had.

As described in other chapters in this volume, the clear definition of goals and objectives is central to the assessment project. At Missouri, participants felt "there [were] inherent difficulties in the process of formulating goals.... [C]onsensus processing requires shared interests and a long time frame; it was not clear that we had either."

Faculty members at Missouri did come to agreement on their commit-ment to teaching and feminist pedagogy and decided to make that the start-ing point for assessment. The University of Missouri used its first faculty development workshop, led by Pat Hutchings, to discuss how materials regu-larly incorporated into women's studies classes—journals, projects, and pa-pers—could form a basis for assessment. As the project progressed, Missouri realized that there were other sources of information easily available, such as course evaluations collected in all women's studies classes.

They also attempted to retrieve other valuable data regularly collected elsewhere on campus but ran into problems with access. They noted that, even if they had had access to data, they did not have the resources necessary to successfully analyze such data—limitations true for other project sites as well. The Missouri report is particularly straightforward in this regard:

> We were not very successful in executing the quantitative part of our project, and we want to note here the sheer difficulty we had getting information from "already existing sources." Quantitative data, such as the kind the registrar has about all students, would have been very useful, but we found it virtually inaccessible. Assessment projects…might do well to think about their own record keeping…. We also underestimated the difficulty of ana-lyzing data….

WELLESLEY COLLEGE
"Stay close to your own strategies and beliefs."
Wellesley College was the only women's college of the participating campus-es and focused its project on that difference, asking, "What makes women's studies at a women's liberal arts college different?"

> [D]id [women's studies] change or affect student's personal lives, their intellectual life, or their political beliefs? Did students feel pressure to give 'politically correct' answers and to only identify with 'feminist' ideas…. We were interested in the quality of de-bate among students and whether or not discussion and learning continued outside the classroom, and if so, with whom.

Wellesley designed an open-ended questionnaire incorporating these items: "Has this course changed or affected your personal life? Has this course affected your intellectual life? Did it change your political beliefs? If so, how?" (See page 93.) In order to examine the difference women's studies courses make, Wellesley administered questionnaires to students in women's

'Our findings demonstrate the limitations of relying on quantitative evaluative data; the qualitative answers gave us a deeper sense of how we might begin to "count" the meanings of our students' responses'

---

studies courses and closely corresponding non-women's studies courses (control courses) and administered them near the end of the semester so students would have more information. Wellesley based its findings on a return of 441 questionnaires—68 percent from women's studies classes and 32 percent from the control courses (only 4 percent of the surveys were from women's studies majors). Wellesley also used an interview guide for majors and alumnae of the women's studies program, and a random sample of alumnae were interviewed by telephone. Both quantitative and qualitative data were collected. However, according to Wellesley's report:

> [O]ur findings demonstrate the limitations of relying on quantitative evaluative data and the ways they "flatten" human experiences. Even when the quantitative answers were statistically similar between the women's studies and control courses, careful reading of the actual answers suggest the *meanings* of the answers varied widely between the women's studies and control courses. Thus, the qualitative answers told us much more about what was really happening in the courses and gave us a deeper sense of how we might begin to "count" the meanings of our students' responses.

As with the other campuses, the project had a significant effect on the Wellesley program. Their report claimed the project made it possible "to make self-conscious what is for many of us unconscious.... [W]e discovered joint problems...in the classrooms, expressed concern about both silences and pressures, and became particularly aware of the difficulties facing our colleagues of color." In addition, project participants learned that "the pressure of the student evaluation questionnaires [has] kept faculty, especially junior faculty, fearful of innovation and controversy in their classrooms."

CONCLUSION

Wellesley College's report included the following quote from a women's studies student: "I will continue to question my beliefs and I will continue to try to educate myself." After their three-year experience with this assessment project, the seven institutions would probably express something similar. As Oberlin College concluded:

> As we continue our discussions regarding long range planning and the future of the Women's Studies Program...we will build our future based on insights generated by ["The Courage to Question"]. In our original assessment design, we claimed that we intended to investigate 'some of the distinctions and tensions, as well as the

commonalities, among students and faculty of diverse racial, ethnic, class, gender and sexual identities.' Three years later, this
statement continues to challenge and engage.

POINTS TO REMEMBER

The research, contributions, and perspectives of members of the National
Assessment Team (NATs) are well documented throughout this book. The
"practical tips" below are brief and informal. They are meant simply as re-
minders of what is stated in much more detail elsewhere.

BEFORE YOU BEGIN ASSESSMENT
► Begin with what you do already.
► Let students participate in the process.
► Determine your community's "passionate questions."
► Take time to conceptualize what you want to know.
► Be sure the process involves diverse campus/student voices, and give voice
  to those who may not otherwise be heard.
► Use surveys and documents developed by people *involved*.
► Use multiple measures in gathering data.
► Pick and choose among diverse methods, and do what you have time for.
► Aim for unobtrusive ways to evaluate.
► Look for alternative ways to do analysis—narrative, conversation,
  dialogue.
► All assessment techniques are not necessarily appropriate to all situations
  or all institutions.
► Think about longitudinal studies: students who graduated, faculty mem-
  bers who have been there a long time, oral histories, and so on.
► Pay attention to how information will be used and who the audience is.
► Remember to think about the variety of places where learning occurs.
  Learning takes place *outside* the classroom as well as in it.
► Ground your exploration in feminist perspectives, and stay close to your
  own strategies and beliefs.
► Be clear in your mind that assessment is not final but ongoing.

ONCE THE ASSESSMENT PROJECT HAS BEGUN
► Think about creative use of staff time—a senior project for a major, gradu-
  ate student project, an internship, and so on.
► Pick a plan you can do.

▶ Have consonance between resources and contribution.
▶ Rely on data already there or that you can obtain easily.
▶ Remember: You do not have to answer every question you ask.
▶ Return to excess data later as time and staffing permit.
▶ Interpret data from several viewpoints over time.
▶ Consider assessment as a movie—not a snapshot—with different angles, different cameras, and reviewed over time.

CONSIDER THE FOLLOWING AS SOURCES OF INFORMATION FOR ASSESSMENT

▶ Journals, papers, reports, diaries
▶ Major committee reports
▶ Syllabi, mid-term exams, final exams, course evaluations
▶ Enrollment trends
▶ Classroom observations
▶ Attendance at optional events
▶ Library check out/reserve lists
▶ Faculty appointment books
▶ Student newspapers
▶ Program newsletters
▶ Brochures, prizes, awards
▶ Audio/visual tapes of classes
▶ Faculty publications
▶ Minutes from meetings
▶ Letters of complaints, grievances, thanks
▶ Student publications
▶ Student presentations
▶ Annual reports
▶ Faculty searches
▶ Grant proposals

APPENDIX A

———■———

SAMPLE INSTRUMENTS

STUDENT QUESTIONNAIRE
UNIVERSITY OF COLORADO

Provide three responses to each question below:

A. answer in regard to courses from your major area of study
B. answer in regard to courses from outside your major area of study
C. answer in regard to this course

1. *On the average*, how often do you miss class sessions?

	Never	Rarely	Occasionally	Frequently	Always
A.	1	2	3	4	5
B.	1	2	3	4	5
C.	1	2	3	4	5

2. What is the usual reason for missing class?
A.
B.
C.

3. How many fellow students do you usually know by name?

	None	A Few	About Half	Most	All
A.	1	2	3	4	5
B.	1	2	3	4	5
C.	1	2	3	4	5

4. How often do you meet with fellow students outside of class?

	Always	Never	Rarely	Occasionally	Frequently
A.	1	2	3	4	5
B.	1	2	3	4	5
C.	1	2	3	4	5

5. What is the usual purpose of meeting with students outside of class?

A.

B.

C.

6. How many fellow students would you say you have friendships with?

	None	A Few	About Half	Most	All
A.	1	2	3	4	5
B.	1	2	3	4	5
C.	1	2	3	4	5

7. How often do you think about or "mull over" course or course related material outside of class (other than for class preparation or for class assignments)?

	Never	Rarely	Occasionally	Frequently	Always
A.	1	2	3	4	5
B.	1	2	3	4	5
C.	1	2	3	4	5

8. How often do you discuss aspects of the course material with someone outside of class?

	Never	Rarely	Occasionally	Frequently	Always
A.	1	2	3	4	5
B.	1	2	3	4	5
C.	1	2	3	4	5

9. With whom do you generally have these discussions? (e.g., friends, mother, roommate, etc.)

A.

B.

C.

10. How often does course content motivate you to do additional reading?

	Never	Rarely	Occasionally	Frequently	Always
A.	1	2	3	4	5
B.	1	2	3	4	5
C.	1	2	3	4	5

11. How often do you find yourself getting "interested" in the course material?

	Never	Rarely	Occasionally	Frequently	Always
A.	1	2	3	4	5
B.	1	2	3	4	5
C.	1	2	3	4	5

12. How often do you find yourself getting "absorbed" in the course material?

	Never	Rarely	Occasionally	Frequently	Always
A.	1	2	3	4	5
B.	1	2	3	4	5
C.	1	2	3	4	5

13. How often does course content relate to you personally?

	Never	Rarely	Occasionally	Frequently	Always
A.	1	2	3	4	5
B.	1	2	3	4	5
C.	1	2	3	4	5

14. How often in the classroom does it feel acceptable to relate course material to your personal life?

	Never	Rarely	Occasionally	Frequently	Always
A.	1	2	3	4	5
B.	1	2	3	4	5
C.	1	2	3	4	5

15. How often do you feel "encouraged" by the instructor to relate course material to your personal life?

	Never	Rarely	Occasionally	Frequently	Always
A.	1	2	3	4	5
B.	1	2	3	4	5
C.	1	2	3	4	5

16. How often in the classroom do you verbally express a personal connection to course content?

	Never	Rarely	Occasionally	Frequently	Always
A.	1	2	3	4	5
B.	1	2	3	4	5
C.	1	2	3	4	5

17. How often does course content actually affect you or your life in some significant way?

	Never	Rarely	Occasionally	Frequently	Always
A.	1	2	3	4	5
B.	1	2	3	4	5
C.	1	2	3	4	5

18. Describe how course content has affected you or your life?
A.
B.
C.

19. In the space below or on the back, write any additional comments you might have regarding any of the question(s) in this questionnaire.

20. Age:

21. Sex: Female/Male

22. Which one of the following race groups do you identify with and feel you belong to?
1. American Indian
2. Black (or Afro American)
3. Hispanic (or Mexican American/Chicano, etc.)
4. Asian (or Oriental)
5. Anglo (or Caucasian)

23. How much education was completed by your parent who went to school longer?
1. junior high
2. high school
3. vocational/technical
4. college (4 year degree)
5. graduate school (doctor, lawyer, Ph.D., etc.)

24. In which social class would you say that your family is located?
1. lower class
2. working class
3. middle class

4. upper middle class
5. upper class

25. Your current student classification:
1. Freshman
2. Sophomore
3. Junior
4. Senior
5. Unclassified

26. Your academic major: _____
    Second major/certificate: _____

27. If you would be willing to participate in further discussion regarding your learning experiences at the University of Colorado, please list your name, current address, and permanent address below.

STUDENT QUESTIONNAIRE
LEWIS AND CLARK COLLEGE

Male:
Female:
Age:
Year in School:
Major:
Minor:

Part I: Gender Studies Program

1. What do you think are the objectives of the Gender Studies Program at Lewis and Clark?

2. How well do you believe these objectives are being met? (What particular strengths and weaknesses do you perceive?)

3. What difference, if any, do you see between a gender studies program and a women's studies program?

4. What impact, if any, do you believe the gender studies program has had on Lewis and Clark?

5. In your opinion, should Lewis and Clark have a gender studies program? Why or why not?

Part II: Gender Studies Core Courses

1. Indicate which, if any, of the following gender studies core courses you have completed and in which courses you are currently enrolled:
C = completed course E = enrolled course
[list of courses followed on original questionnaire]

2. Circle the number on the scale that best represents your overall learning in the above gender studies core courses:

1	2	3	4	5
poor	fair	average	good	excellent

3. What do you consider to be your most significant and least significant learning experiences in these courses?

4. How do these gender studies core courses compare with other courses you have taken at Lewis and Clark?

5. Was the learning/teaching climate in these gender studies core courses different from your non-gender studies classes? If so, how?

6. What effect, if any, have these gender studies core courses had on your understanding of issues of gender, race, and class?

7. Which of these courses would you recommend to other students? Why?

Part III: Practicum/Internship in Gender Studies

If you completed or are currently involved in a practicum/internship in gender studies, describe the practicum and comment on the experience:

Part IV: Other Courses with a Gender Focus

1. What other courses have you taken in the Lewis and Clark general college curriculum that included a focus on gender issues?

2. Circle the number on the scale that best represents your overall learning in these courses:

1	2	3	4	5
poor	fair	average	good	excellent

3. What do you consider to be your most significant and least significant learning experience in these courses?

4. How do these courses compare with other courses you have taken at Lewis and Clark?

5. Which of these courses would you recommend to other students? Why?

Part V: Gender and Overseas Programs

1. Have you participated in a Lewis and Clark overseas program?   Yes   No
   If yes, what was the program?

2. How did gender issues figure in the program—in preparation, during the course of the overseas study, after return to campus?

Part VI: Gender Studies Symposium

1. Have you ever attended any of the Lewis and Clark Gender Studies Symposium events? Yes   No
   If yes, circle the year(s) of your participation in the symposium?
       1982   1983   1984   1985   1986   1987   1988   1989   1990

2. Which events do you recall attending, and what was your evaluation?

3. What effect did your attendance at the symposium have on your understanding of issues of gender, race, and class?

4. Circle the number of the scale that best represents your learning experience in the symposium?

1	2	3	4	5
poor	fair	average	good	excellent

5. Have you ever been involved as a planner, presenter, or moderator in a Lewis and Clark Gender Studies Symposium?

Yes   No

If yes, circle the year(s) of your participation:

1982   1983   1984   1985   1986   1987   1988   1989   1990

6. Describe and comment on your participation in the symposium:

7. What effect did your participation in the symposium have on your understanding of issues of gender, race, and class?

8. Circle the number of the scale that best represents your learning experience as a symposium planner, presenter, and/or moderator:

1	2	3	4	5
poor	fair	average	good	excellent

Part VII: What Else?

What else would you like to communicate to us about the Gender Studies Program at Lewis and Clark as we plan for the future?

CHARACTERISTICS OF CONNECTED AND SEPARATE KNOWING

Aspect	Connected Knowing	Separate Knowing
The name of the game:	The "Believing Game": looking for what is right—accepting	The "Doubting Game": looking for what is wrong—critical
Goals:	To construct meaning—to understand and to be understood	To construct truth—to prove, disprove, and convince
The relationship between the knowers:	Collaborative: reasons *with* the other	Adversarial: reasoning *against* the other

Aspect	Connected Knowing	Separate Knowing
The knower's relationship to the known:	Attachment & closeness	Detachment & distance
The nature of agency:	Active surrender	Mastery and control
The nature of discourse:	Narrative & contextual	Logical & abstract
The role of emotion:	Feelings illuminate thought	Feelings cloud thought
Procedure for transcending subjectivity:	"Objectivity" achieved by adopting the other's perspective	"Objectivity" achieved by adhering to impersonal and universal standards
Basis of authority:	Commonality of experience	Mastery of relevant knowledge and methodology
Strengths:	Expansive, inclusive	Narrowing, discriminating
Vulnerabilities:	Loss of identity and autonomy	Alienation and absence of care

Based on Belenky, Clinchy, Goldberger, & Tarule, *Women's Ways of Knowing: The Development of Self, Voice, & Mind* (New York: Basic Books, Inc., 1986); and Elbow, *Writing Without Teachers* (New York: Cambridge University Press, 1973), with thanks to Hilarie Davis for her suggestions.

LEWIS AND CLARK
SCORING SHEET
FOR KNOWLEDGE BASE
AND LEARNING SKILLS

Reader _____ File _____
Paper _____
Date _____ Female _____ Male _____

I. Plots for Knowledge Base for Gender Studies

____ 1. **Politics of sex/gender plot** (economic, political and sexual subjugation of women built into social structures; activism for change)

____ 2. **Cultural images of sex/gender plot** (representations of gender—masculinity and femininity—in art and the media, both high and mass culture)

___ 3. **Nature/nurture plot** (biological to socially learned differences)

___ 4. **Diversity plot** (recognition and respect for racial, ethnic, cultural, sexual, class, and age differences)

___ 5. **Body plot** (female sexuality and male sexuality; heterosexuality and homosexuality)

___ 6. **Communication plot** (verbal and nonverbal; discursive and nondiscursive; the making and authorization of meaning)

___ 7. **Interpersonal relationships plot** (the structuring, maintenance, and termination of dyadic relationships, family relationships, work relationships, and other small group relationships, etc.)

___ 8. **Women's creation of knowledge plot** (women's contribution throughout the disciplines to the creation of knowledge)

II. Learning Skills

___ 1. Social construction of gender

    1   2   3   4   5

___ 2. Agency of the oppressed

    1   2   3   4   5

___ 3. Form and content: questioning adequacy of traditional forms of expressions; experimentation with non-traditional forms

    1   2   3   4   5

___ 4. Knowledge in gender studies seen as interminable; producing rather than repeating knowledge

    1   2   3   4   5

___ 5. Positionality—self-awareness, self-empowerment, "clicks," and "epiphanies"

    1   2   3   4   5

___ 6. Social construction of knowledge

    1   2   3   4   5

STUDENT QUESTIONNAIRE
OLD DOMINION UNIVERSITY

Name:
Social Security Number:
Women's studies major/minor:
Course name and number:
Instructor:
Number of students in the class:

1. Style of teaching:
☐ all lecture
☐ lecture and students' questions/comments
☐ lecture and discussion
☐ mostly discussion

2. Does the instructor recommend or require group discussion or group projects?

3. Currently, how many students do you know in class (including acquaintances and friends)?
___ number of female acquaintances and friends
___ number of male acquaintances and friends

4. Currently how many students in class are friends?
    female friends / male friends

5. Currently how many students in class are close, personal friends?
    female close friends / male close friends

6. Think of the person whom you know *best* in this class. Check all of the following activities that apply to your interactions with this person:
☐ I see her/him only in class.
☐ I see her/him before and/or after classes but only at ODU.
☐ I see her/him for social occasions away from ODU.
☐ I talk with her/him outside of class about course assignments.
☐ I talk with her/him outside of class about topics mentioned or discussed in class.

7. How did being in class together change (if it did) your relationship with this person?

ALUMNAE QUESTIONNAIRE
OLD DOMINION UNIVERSITY

INTRODUCTION: In order to learn more about Old Dominion University's Women's Studies Program and its impact on students, we ask that you respond to the following questions. We are interested in anything and everything that you have to share with us about your women's studies experiences, but feel free to skip questions that are not relevant to your situation. Women's studies include all cross-listed courses, not just WMST courses.

Background Information

1. What year did you graduate?

2. What is your age?

3. What is your race/ethnicity?

4. What was your major?

5. After leaving ODU did you earn any advanced degree(s)? In what fields?

6. Are you currently earning any advanced degree? In what field? Please provide us with an employment and volunteer activity history:

7a. First job (since graduation from ODU); number of years at the job

7b. Second job; number of years at the job

7c. Third job; number of years at the job

8. List volunteer activities since graduating from ODU

9. How were the learning environments structured in your women's studies courses (e.g., lecture, small group discussions, group projects)?

10. Did the size of the class make a difference? If so, how?

11. Were the learning environments different from non-women's studies courses? If so, how?

12. Was there much discussion in women's studies classes? Did students debate or argue with each other? Did you feel that your voice was heard and respected? If not, why not?

13. Did you discuss course readings and lectures outside the classroom? If so, with whom? (specify relationship: roommates, female friends, male friends, family)

14. Were different points of view encouraged by the instructors in your courses? If so, how did instructors teach you about different points of view? (give examples)

15. Did you participate in women's studies activities other than courses? If so, describe these and their impact on you.

16. How did your participation in the women's studies program make you feel about yourself?

We are interested in all of your thoughts and feelings about the women's studies program and its courses at ODU. Please share any other thoughts you have.

STUDENT QUESTIONNAIRE
WELLESLEY COLLEGE

This questionnaire is part of a national study being done by Wellesley's Women's Studies Program. We are asking students in selected women's studies and non-women's studies courses to answer this brief questionnaire. Your answers should reflect your experience in the class where you received this survey. Your name is not requested and your professor will not see the survey. We deeply appreciate your time.

Directions
If a question does not apply, please write "not applicable." If you do not have an answer or don't know, please write "don't know."

Course number and name: _____

Background Information
1. What year do you expect to graduate?

2. What is your age?

3. What is your race/ethnicity?

4. What is your major? What is your minor?

5. After graduation are you planning to attend graduate or professional school?
        Yes   No   Don't know   [circle one]
In what fields? [specify degrees and fields]

Questions About This Course

1. How has this course changed or affected your personal life?

2. How has this course affected your intellectual life?

3. Did it change your political beliefs? If so, how?

4. How was the learning environment structured in the classroom? (e.g., lecture only, lecture and discussion, student led, sat in a circle, etc.)

5. How does the learning environment in this class compare to any courses you have taken in women's studies? (Women's studies courses and courses cross-listed in women's studies can be used as comparisons.)

6. Is there much discussion in this class?

7. Do students debate or argue among one another? [provide examples]

8. How often did you discuss course readings and lectures outside the classroom?
        Constantly   Occasionally   Rarely   [circle one]
        Only when studying for an exam   Never
If so, with whom? [specify relationship: roommates, female friends, male friends, family]

9. Do you feel there is pressure to give "politically correct" answers?

Yes   No   [circle one]

If yes, please explain your answer.

10. Were different points of view encouraged by the professor?

Yes   No   Sometimes   [circle one]

11. In terms of course content, did you learn how to think about an issue or social problem from different political or theoretical points of view? [give examples]

12. Do you feel that you will apply what you learned in this class to your work and/or further education?

Yes   No   Don't know   [circle one]

If yes, how?

SURVEY OF PARTICIPANTS IN INTRODUCTION TO WOMEN'S STUDIES CUNY–HUNTER COLLEGE

PART I:

1. Your year at Hunter:
___ first-year student
___ sophomore
___ junior
___ senior

2. Your sex: ___ Female   ___ Male

3. How do you identify yourself in terms of your ethnic identity?

4. Your age:
___ 15–20
___ 21–30
___ 31–40
___ 41–50
___ 51–60
___ 61–70
___ 71+

5. Your major: _____

Your co-major or minor: _____

6. Why did you take "Introduction to Women's Studies"? (check all that apply)

___ A friend recommended it

___ It was one of the few open at the time I wanted

___ I wanted to take a/another women's studies course

___ I am a women's studies collateral major

___ I am thinking about becoming a women's studies collateral major

___ The subject matter intrigued me

___ I wanted to take a course with this professor

___ Other (please list)

7. Additional information about yourself you would like to share with us:

PART II:

We would like to know the ways the introductory course has had an impact on you. The following questions deal with this issue.

1. Comment on the value of this course to you as a whole.

2. If you had to describe this course to a friend, what three adjectives would you use? Why?

3. Did this course meet your expectations? Why or why not?

4. If the instructor of this course could have done something differently, what would that have been?

5. If you could have done something differently in this course, what would that have been?

6. Please suggest three topics you believe need to be discussed in the introductory course.

7. Compared to other introductory courses you have taken (e.g., introductory sociology, introductory psychology), how has "Introduction to Women's Studies" been similar?

8. Was there a balance between the survey-scope of the course and some more in-depth investigation? Please explain.

9. Please identify three major themes from the introductory course in women's studies.

10. Do you think that a sense of community was built in your introductory course? Why or why not?

11. What readings did you find particularly useful in this course? Why?

12. This is your space! We welcome your comments about any of the items in the survey and additional information about the introductory course you would like to share with us. Thank you again.

FACULTY QUESTIONNAIRE
OBERLIN COLLEGE

1. Some of the goals of Oberlin's Women's Studies Program are:
☐ student self-empowerment
☐ recognition of differences
☐ collaborative learning
☐ understanding the relationship between race, class, gender, and sexuality.
Which of these goals do you consider most important? Are there others you would add?

2. Which of the following activities in your opinion are the most important to the future of the Women's Studies Program? Please rank from 1=least important to 7=most important.
____ change program status to department
____ raise funds from alumni to create an endowed chair in women's studies
____ lobby administration and trustees for more support, financial and otherwise, for the program
____ improve the representation of women of color on the faculty and staff and among students
____ increase the visibility of the program
____ address questions of difference and diversity within the women's studies curriculum
____ increase number of full-time faculty (currently one person)

3. What impact do you think the Women's Studies Program has on Oberlin College?

4. What significant learning experiences do you think women's studies courses offer students?

5. Do you believe that women's studies courses differ in pedagogy—in how students learn—from non-women's studies courses?
    Yes   No   If yes, how?

6. Have you ever taught a course that was cross-listed with women's studies? Yes   No

7. Have you ever taught a women's studies-related course?   Yes   No

8. Do you include any of the following perspectives in the courses you teach, whether or not they are women's studies courses? Perspectives on:
☐ Gender
☐ Class
☐ Race
☐ Sexuality
    (most of the time, some of the time, rarely, never)

9. Do you ever approach your subject with an integrative analysis of gender, race, class, and sexuality?
Yes   No   (Please explain)

10. Which of the following teaching techniques do you use?
☐ lectures by teacher
☐ presentations by individual students
☐ discussions led by teacher
☐ discussions led by individual students
☐ discussions led by groups of students
☐ other:

11. Are you faculty or administration?

12. How many years have you taught at Oberlin?

13. Do you teach in the conservatory or the college?

14. In what division of the college do you teach?

15. Are you female or male?

16. What is your race/ethnicity?

17. We welcome your comments about the Women's Studies Program as we plan for the future.

OBERLIN STUDENT SELF-STATEMENTS

Student Self-Statement #1

1. Do you expect this class to address questions of race?
   Do you expect this class to address questions of gender?
   Do you expect this class to address questions of sexuality?
   Do you expect this class to address questions of social class?

2. Do you expect this class to take a feminist approach? What does this mean for you? For example, does it mean:
   a. inclusion of women authors, artists, scientists, etc., in the syllabus
   b. discussions of systems of race, gender, and class
   c. an analysis of power relations in terms of hierarchy, oppression, and exploitation
   d. other:

3. What kind of learning environment do you expect? For example, only lecture, only discussion, both lectures and discussion, student-led discussion, faculty led discussion? other?

4. What kind of learning environment do you prefer or learn best in?

5. If you expect discussion, do you expect to be actively engaged in discussion or do you expect the teacher to lead most of the discussion?

6. What do you hope to learn in this class?

Student Self-Statement #2

1. Does this class address questions of race? How?
   Does this class address questions of gender? How?
   Does this class address questions of sexuality? How?

Does this class address questions of social class? How?

2. Is this class taking a feminist approach? Please explain.

3. Collaborative learning is defined as a pedagogical style that emphasizes cooperative efforts among students and faculty members. It is rooted in the belief that learning is social in nature and stresses common inquiry as a basic learning process. Do
you think collaborative learning has taken place in your classroom? In what specific
ways?

4. Since true collaborative learning means working with and learning from people
who are different from oneself, how have you negotiated and mediated those
differences?

5. What are some of the significant things you are learning in this class?

Student Self-Statement #3
1.   Has this class addressed questions of race?   How?
     Has this class addressed questions of gender? How?
     Has this class addressed questions of sexuality? How?
     Has this class addressed questions of social class? How?

2. How would you characterize the most important things you have learned in this
class (in terms of content and process)?

SENIOR SEMINAR PEER INTERVIEW
OBERLIN COLLEGE

Instructions
1. Please audiotape the entire interview, and turn in the cassettes with your summary
of the interview.
2. I expect you to spend about 45 minutes on each interview.
3. Be sure you ask the questions listed below, but feel free to add questions. While
this will help the Program with the NWSA/FIPSE Assessment Project, I also want you
to be able to make sense of your WOST experiences for yourselves.
4. Write up a five-page report, summarizing the responses of the person you interview. Do not transcribe the tape but use direct quotes in your summary. Organize the
summary in terms of the questions below, or in terms of categories that emerge from
your conversation/interview.

Peer Interview Questions

1. How did you become a WOST major?

2. Summarize what you consider to be your most important "learning" as a WOST major. What did you take from WOST to other classes?

3. Can you identify one or two significant experiences at Oberlin (a course, an event, a professor, friendships, membership in political organizations, etc.) that most influenced your feminist consciousness?

4. Briefly describe changes in your expectations of the content and process of your WOST education from the time you were a freshperson through your senior year.

5. How has WOST affected your intellectual life, your political beliefs, and your personal life? Please describe any other significant changes.

6. Goals of the Oberlin WOST Program include self empowerment; recognition of differences; collaborative learning; understanding interdisciplinary connections in the analysis of gender, race, class, and sexuality; and linking personal with social responsibility. Which of these goals are most important to you and which do you feel you have accomplished as a student in WOST?

7. Which of the following activities do you consider most important for the future of WOST at Oberlin. Please rank in order of importance (1 = most important):
___ Change status from program to department.
___ Increase number of full-time faculty members in WOST.
___ Increase visibility of program within and outside the college.
___ Raise funds from alumni/ae to create endowed chair in WOST.
___ Improve representation of women of color on faculty, among students and staff, and in the curriculum.
___ Lobby administration and trustees for more support for program.

8. What kinds of things (jobs, further education, communities) are you looking for after graduation? How does being a WOST student influence your quest?

9. Is there anything else you want to add about what it has meant to be a WOST major at Oberlin? Can you identify gaps in your experience as a major? What needs improvement?

ASSESSMENT MATRIX FOR KEY QUESTIONS*
AT LEWIS AND CLARK COLLEGE

Methods Used	Q1–Gender Analysis	Q2–Institutional Climate	Q3–Personal Growth
Course Evaluations	X	X	X
Syllabi	X	**X**	
Computer Conversations	X		X
Student Papers	**X**	**X**	
Symposium Programs	X	**X**	
Symposium Papers	X	X	
Questionnaires Student Alumni Faculty	X X X	**X** **X** **X**	**X** **X** **X**
Journals Diaries	X	X	X
Honors Projects	X	X	
Practica	X	X	X

*Bold face type indicates primary sources of information for each question.

APPENDIX B

———— ∎ ————

DIRECTORY OF CONSULTANTS

The following list of consultants consists only of those people who were involved in the "Courage to Question" project. The names include two groups: individuals who were part of the National Assessment Team advising participants about assessment and women's studies faculty members from participating institutions who had gained expertise and would have time to assist other campuses in assessment projects. We have highlighted specializations and strengths to facilitate matching the consultant to meet specific needs of a campus assessment project.

———————————

CAROLYNE W. ARNOLD
Assistant Professor
College of Public and Community Services
University of Massachusetts–Boston
Boston, Massachusetts 02125

National Assessment Team Member
Carolyne Arnold, who also is a senior researcher at the Wellesley College Center for Research on Women, has conducted a number of evaluation research and assessment studies and has extensive experience in the application of a range of quantitative as well as qualitative methods and techniques. Her skills include the conceptualization of research designs and methodologies, sample selection, survey and questionnaire construction, interviewing techniques, participant observation, social science experiments, reduction and interpretation of data, and related facets of investigation. Her area of expertise is minority women and the epidemiology of reproductive biology.

ANITA CLAIR FELLMAN
Director, Women's Studies Program
Associate Professor of History
Old Dominion University
BAL 809
Hampton Boulevard
Norfolk, Virginia 23529

Anita Clair Fellman co-authored "Making Connections" in *The Courage to Question: Women's Studies and Student Learning*. Her field of specialization is American history. Her publications include *Rethinking Canada: The Promise of Women's History*; "Laura Ingalls Wilder and Rose Wilder Lane: The Politics of a Mother-Daughter Relationship"; and "The Literature of Individualism: The *Little House* Books in American Culture" (forthcoming). Her strengths in assessment are in setting realistic goals; assessing the knowledge base, especially in women's studies; and creating strategies for building cohesive investigative teams.

LAURIE ANN FINKE
Director, Women's and Gender Studies Program
Kenyon College
Gambier, Ohio 43022

Laurie Ann Finke, formerly a faculty member at Lewis and Clark College, is the co-author of "A Single Curriculum" in *The Courage to Question*. Her fields of specialization include theory, feminist theory, and gender studies. Her strengths as assessment consultant include portfolio assessment, design of assessment tools, and curriculum integration and its assessment. Finke's publications include *Feminist Theory, Women's Writing: The Uses of Complexity*; and "Pedagogy of the Depressed: Feminism, Poststructuralism, and Pedagogic Practice" (forthcoming).

PAT HUTCHINGS
Director, AAHE Teaching Initiative
American Association for Higher Education
One Dupont Circle, Suite 360
Washington, D.C. 20036

National Assessment Team Member and project external evaluator Pat
Hutchings formerly was the director of AAHE's Assessment Forum, which
promotes approaches to assessment that involve faculty members and foster
more and better student learning. She is the author of numerous articles on
creative teaching and assessment, including "Watching Assessment: Questions, Stories, Prospects" and "Learning Over Time: Portfolio Assessment."
She has worked with hundreds of faculty members on teaching, learning, and
assessment. Hutchings' strengths as an assessment consultant include working on the early stages of a project, where a group comes to understand what
assessment, at its best, might do for them and their program. She also is
helpful with questions such as: Who is doing what on campuses across the
country? What seems to be working when it comes to contributing to student learning? Who are the people to talk to for special advice?

LEE KNEFELKAMP
Chair, Higher Education Department
Professor of Higher Education
P.O. Box 101
Teachers College, Columbia University
New York, New York 10027

Chair, National Assessment Team
Lee Knefelkamp's areas of expertise include: intellectual and ethical development in both traditional and women's models/methods of assessment; help-
ing faculty members create and use "cues" (phrases, language structure) to
assess this type of development; and differentiating learning styles, using
Myers-Briggs, Kolb, and other models of differences in learning styles. She
also has expertise in the construction of questionnaires and interview formats and recording of information. Knefelkamp is skilled at creating "decision rules" that groups use to view contextually specific data such as exams,

papers, presentations; personal/interpersonal development; and finding ways
to assess interpersonal growth dynamics. Finally, she has experience working
with portfolios, assessment of experiential learning, exam questions,
short/quick classroom assessment techniques, and participant observation.

CARYN McTIGHE MUSIL
Senior Research Associate
Association of American Colleges
1818 R Street, N.W.
Washington, D.C. 20009

*Project Director, "The Courage to Question: Women's Studies and Student
Learning"*
Caryn McTighe Musil is the editor of three publications emerging from
"The Courage to Question." She formerly was the executive director of the
National Women's Studies Association. Musil was chair of the Women's
Studies National Task Force that wrote *Liberal Learning and the Women's
Studies Major* and is the author of numerous articles and presentations on
women's studies, assessment, curriculum transformation, and student learning. She has served as a consultant and external evaluator at more than a
dozen colleges and universities. Musil's special expertise is in women's studies
program development, curriculum development, faculty development, and
pedagogy. Her strengths in assessment include: "detoxifying" the term, getting started on a project, identifying potential sources of data collections,
constructing an inclusive assessment design, and using research findings
strategically for program development and improvement.

MICHELE PALUDI

Professor of Psychology
Hunter College, City University of New York
695 Park Avenue
New York, New York 10021

Michele Paludi, formerly director of Hunter's Women's Studies Program, is
the co-author of "Feminist Education" in *The Courage to Question*. Her field
of specialization is experimental psychology, with an emphasis on career development concerns. Paludi's strengths as assessment consultant include developing surveys and establishing assessment workshops for faculty members
and administrators. Her publications include *Foundations for a Feminist
Restructuring of the Academic Disciplines*; *Exploring/Teaching the Psychology of
Women: A Manual of Resources*; and "Integrating the Scholarship on Ethnicity into the Psychology of Women Course."

JOAN POLINER SHAPIRO

Associate Dean, College of Education
Ritter Hall, 2nd Floor
Temple University
Philadelphia, Pennsylvania 19122

National Assessment Team Member
Joan Poliner Shapiro, who was for many years co-director of the women's
studies program at the University of Pennsylvania, is the author of numerous
articles on evaluation and assessment, including, "Participatory Evaluation:
Towards a Transformation of Assessment for Women's Studies Programs and
Projects" and "Consideration of Ethical Issues in the Assessment of Feminist
Projects: A Case Study Using Illuminative Evaluation." She possesses a
background in evaluating both quantitative and qualitative assessment approaches and has helped design questionnaires and interview formats for
feminist projects. She calls her particular form of assessment "participatory
evaluation." Shapiro has served as external evaluator at many diverse higher
educational sites including, among others, Bryn Mawr College, Great Lakes
Colleges at the University of Michigan, and the University of Delaware.

LINDA R. SILVER
Coordinator, Women's Studies Program
Oberlin College
Oberlin, Ohio 44074

Linda Silver is the author of "Self-Empowerment and Difference" in *The Courage to Question*. Her field of specialization is public administration and librarianship, and she has had assessment experience at Oberlin College, Cleveland State University, and Cuyahoga County Public Library. Silver's experience best corresponds to assessment activities within interdisciplinary academic programs or public organizations with more than four hundred employees.

JILL MATTUCK TARULE
Dean of the College of Education and Social Services
University of Vermont
311 Waterman Building
Burlington, Vermont 05405-0160

National Assessment Team Member
One of the authors of *Women's Ways of Knowing*, Jill Mattuck Tarule is interested in assessment emphasizing qualitative research and formative evaluation. Tarule is experienced with all aspects of interviewing (design of interview schedule, training interviewers, data analysis), including that which incorporates exploring cognitive reasoning and other developmental themes. She places particular emphasis on how women as learners have distinct needs that frequently are not addressed by mainstream academic cultures. Tarule has worked with instruments other than interviews and can consult on the use of the Kolb Learning Style Inventory, Loevinger's Ego Development Scale, and student self-evaluations. She also has done a number of program evaluations using a qualitative narrative approach and creates designs sensitive to sociopolitical issues within an institution.

MARY KAY THOMPSON TETREAULT
Dean, School of Human Development and Community Service
California State University–Fullerton
Fullerton, California 92634

National Assessment Team Member
Mary Kay Thompson Tetreault is co-author of *Inside Women's Classrooms: Mastery, Voice, Authority and Positionality* (forthcoming). She is the author of numerous articles in education and women's studies journals, including "Integrating Content About Women and Gender Into the Curriculum" and "Inside Feminist Classrooms: An Ethnographic Approach" (forthcoming). Her interests include the ways feminist theory informs the transformation of the disciplines, the evaluation of women's studies courses and curriculum integration projects, and feminist ways of teaching. She can assist in ethnographic approaches to assessment. Tetreault's earlier work included the development of feminist phase theory—a classification scheme that details the evolution in thought during the past twenty years about the incorporation of women's traditions, history, and experiences into selected disciplines.

GAY VICTORIA
Instructor/Research Assistant, Women's Studies Program
University of Colorado
Cottage No. 1, Campus Box 246
Boulder, Colorado 80309-0246

Gay Victoria is the co-author of "Personalized Learning" in *The Courage to Question*. Her field of specialization is feminist pedagogy. Victoria's strengths as an assessment consultant include an ability to identify phenomena that warrant more intensive investigation, or "progressive focusing." Her experience best corresponds to assessment activities within women's studies programs at large institutions, using classroom observation and illuminative evaluation.

JEAN WARD
Director, Gender Studies Program
Professor of Communications
Lewis and Clark College
Portland, Oregon 97219

Jean Ward is the co-author of "A Single Curriculum" in *The Courage to Question*. Her field of specialization is rhetoric and public address. Her strengths as an assessment consultant include curricular integration assessment for women's studies and gender studies, portfolio assessment for women's studies and gender studies, assessment of knowledge base and learning skills in women's studies and gender studies, and the use of interviews in assessment. She has served as a reviewer for FIPSE on grant proposals for projects related to women, minorities, and core curriculum. Ward's presentations include "Incorporating Feminist Scholarship into the Core Curriculum: Model Projects in the Northwest" and "Incorporating Perspectives on Women in the Undergraduate Curriculum: Taking a Close Look." Her experience best corresponds to assessment activities in women's studies or gender studies at private liberal arts colleges, using qualitative and quantitative methodologies.

MARCIA WESTKOTT
Director, Women's Studies Program
Professor of Sociology
University of Colorado
Cottage No. 1, Campus Box 246
Boulder, Colorado 80309-0246

Marcia Westkott is the co-author of "Personalized Learning" in *The Courage to Question*. Her field of specialization is feminist theory and the psychology of women. She has had assessment experience at the University of Colorado, Oregon State University, and Western Washington State University. Westkott's strengths as an assessment consultant include the ability to synthesize information and materials. Her publications include "The New Psychology of Women: A Cautionary View" (forthcoming) and "Women's Studies as a Strategy for Change: Between Criticism and Vision." Her presentations include "Assessing Women's Studies Programs"; "Integrating Women of Color in the Liberal Arts Curriculum"; and "The General Education Requirement." She has served as a consultant to the women's studies program at the University of Arizona, the Women's Studies Integration Project at Colorado College, and the University of Maine.

BARBARA ANN WINSTEAD
Associate Professor of Psychology
Old Dominion University
Hampton Boulevard
Norfolk, Virginia 23529

Barbara Ann Winstead is the co-author of "Making Connections" in *The Courage to Question*. Her field of specialization is personality and developmental psychology. Her presentations include "Assessment of Student Learning in Women's Studies at Old Dominion University"; "Relationship and Achievement Stressors: Sex Differences in Appraisals, Coping, and Outcome"; and "Contemporary Topics in Personality Theory, Research, and Applications: Attachment and Gender." Her strengths in assessment are in setting realistic goals; assessing the knowledge base, especially in women's studies; and creating strategies for building cohesive investigative teams.

APPENDIX C

———■———

SELECTED BIBLIOGRAPHY

BOOKS

Adelman, Clifford. *Performance and Judgment: Essays on Principles and Practice in the Assessment of College Student Learning.* Washington: Office of Educational Research and Improvement, U.S. Department of Education, 1988.

This collection of essays on assessment in higher education is directed toward academic administrators and faculty members. It provides a basis for drafting a charge to an assessment committee, communicating effectively regarding assessment, and evaluating assessment designs.

Astin, Alexander. *Achieving Educational Excellence: A Critical Assessment of Priorities and Practices in Higher Education.* San Francisco: Jossey-Bass, 1985.

Astin's book presents views of the American higher education system and traditional concepts of excellence. It includes examinations of educational equity, student learning and development, and the role of teacher training.

_____. *Assessment for Excellence: The Philosophy and Practice of Assessment and Evaluation in Higher Education.* New York: American Council on Education and Macmillan Company, 1991.

_____. *What Matters in College: Four Critical Years.* San Francisco: Jossey-Bass, 1992.

Banta, Trudy W., ed. *New Directions for Institutional Research,* No. 59. San Francisco: Jossey-Bass, 1988.

Articles within this volume reflect both the benefits of comprehensive assessment programs and their problems. It includes an annotated bibliography and representative assessment programs. The volume also contains "Implementing Outcomes Assessment: Promise and Perils," which examines what students and graduates know and what they are able to do with that knowledge and presents students' perceptions regarding the quality of programs and services.

Belanoff, Pat, and Marcia Dickson, eds. *Portfolios: Process and Product.*
   Portsmouth, N.H.: Boynton/Cook Publishers, 1991.
Focusing on the practical and theoretical approaches of portfolio assessment,
this work offers places to start and covers recent developments in the field of
assessment. One section, "Bridges to Academic Goals: A Look at Returning
Adult Portfolios," includes information on portfolios for proficiency testing,
program assessment, classroom portfolios, and political issues.

Belenky, Mary Field, Blythe McVicker Clinchy, Nancy Rule Goldberger, and
   Jill Mattuck Tarule. *Women's Ways of Knowing: The Development of Self,
   Voice, and Mind.* New York: Basic Books, 1986.
Based on extensive interviews with women, this landmark book examines
five principal ways of knowing developed by women: silence, received knowing, subjective knowing, procedural knowing, and constructed knowing. The
investigation acknowledges the historical and cultural institutions that have
shaped women's intellectual and personal lives.

Boyer, Ernest L. *College: The Undergraduate Experience in America.* New
   York: Harper & Row, 1987.
Boyer's work examines the undergraduate experience and explores how insti-
tutional structures and procedures affect students' lives.

Cross, K. Patricia, and Thomas A. Angelo. *Classroom Assessment Techniques:
   A Handbook for Faculty.* Ann Arbor: National Center for Research to
   Improve Postsecondary Teaching and Learning, University of Michigan,
   1988.
A reference book for ideas and guidance on assessment, this work includes
the following sections: "Techniques for Assessing Academic Skills and
Intellectual Development"; "Techniques for Assessing Students' Self-
Awareness as Learners and Self-Assessments of Learning Skills"; and
"Techniques for Assessing Student Reactions to Teachers and Teaching
Methods, Course Materials, Activities, and Assignments."

_____. *A Handbook for College Teachers.* San Francisco: Jossey-Bass,
   1992.
This volume is designed as a companion to Cross and Angelo's earlier volume, *A Handbook for Faculty.* This new edition, however, is organized with a
focus on various academic disciplines.

Erwin, T. Dary. *Assessing Student Learning and Development*. San Francisco:
     Jossey-Bass, 1991.
A practical guide to designing and implementing strategies for evaluating
the effectiveness of institutional programs and services, this book includes
chapters on "Selecting Assessment Methods" and "Analyzing Information
and Drawing Conclusions." It also contains sample instruments.

Ewell, Peter T. *Assessing Educational Outcomes*. New Directions for
     Institutional Research, No. 47. San Francisco: Jossey-Bass, 1985.
Ewell's work includes an overview of research on student attitudes, achievement, and occupational and career development ("outcomes") and presents
information on the organization and implementation of such programs in
various settings. It also contains basic technical information regarding the
design of studies and use of results.

Ewell, Peter T. and Robert P. Lisensky. *Assessing Institutional Effectiveness*.
     Washington: Consortium for the Advancement of Private Higher
     Education, 1988.
This book includes the authors' observations on their experiences during an
assessment project with selected private liberal arts colleges. It defines learning outcomes and offers ways to determine strategies for measuring them.

Halpern, D. F., ed. *Student Outcomes Assessment: What Institutions Stand to
     Gain*. New Directions for Higher Education, No. 59. San Francisco:
     Jossey-Bass, 1987.
Includes articles exploring a variety of issues and concerns regarding student
outcomes assessment. Four models of assessment are included: the value-
added approach, general-education approach, state-mandated testing, and
incentive funding.

Johnson, Reid, Joseph Prus, Charles J. Andersen, and Elaine El-Khawas.
     *Assessing Assessment: An In-depth Status Report on the Higher Education
     Assessment Movement in 1990*. Washington: American Council on Edu-
     cation, 1991.
This book includes an "overall picture" of assessment and examines faculty
members' roles as well as the perceived benefits and liabilities of assessment.

Magolda, Marcia B. Baxter. *Knowing and Reasoning in College: Gender Related Patterns in Students' Intellectual Development.* San Francisco: Jossey Bass, 1992.

Seidman, E. *In the Words of the Faculty: Perspectives on Improving Teaching and Educational Quality in Community College.* San Francisco: Jossey-Bass, 1985.
Seidman's work examines the context of teaching in a community college and the major issues faculty members face. It presents profiles of community college faculty members and suggests ways institutions can support them.

ARTICLES AND REPORTS
Astin, Alexander. "Assessment as a Tool for Institutional Renewal and Reform." Wolff, Ralph A. "Assessment and Accreditation: A Shotgun Marriage?" In *Assessment 1990: Accreditation and Renewal,* a volume of two presentations from the Fifth American Association for Higher Education Conference on Assessment in Higher Education, 1990.

Brown, Rexford. "You Can't Get There From Here." Ewell, Peter T. "Hearts and Minds: Reflections on the Ideologies of Assessment." Knefelkamp, Lee. "Assessment as Transformation." *Three Presentations: 1989,* a volume of three presentations from the Fourth American Association for Higher Education Conference on Assessment in Higher Education, 1989.

Cross, K. Patricia. "Feedback in the Classroom: Making Assessment Matter." Paper presented at American Association for Higher Education Assessment Forum, Chicago, 1988.
This article examines the use of assessment within the classroom to improve instruction as well as the quality of education.

Davis, B. G. "Demystifying Assessment: Learning from the Field of Evaluation." In *Achieving Assessment Goals Using Evaluation Techniques,* New Directions for Higher Education, No. 67. P.J. Gray, ed. San Francisco: Jossey-Bass, 1989.

Ewell, Peter T. "Assessment: What's It All About." *Change* 17 (November/
    December 1985): 32–36.
Ewell's article contains descriptions of institutional accountability in higher
education based on measuring objective outcomes. It also discusses whether
assessment can be performed objectively and what effects external accountability pressures have on higher education practices.

_____. "Establishing a Campus-Based Assessment Program." In
    D. F. Halpern, ed. *Student Outcomes Assessment: What Institutions Stand
    to Gain.* New Directions for Higher Education, No. 59. San Francisco:
    Jossey-Bass, 1987.
An introduction to assessment. Provides practical information, thoughtful
discussion, and suggestions for implementing an assessment program.

_____. "To Capture the Ineffable: New Forms of Assessment in
    Higher Education," in *Reprise 1991: Reprints of Two Papers Treating
    Assessment's History and Implementation.* Washington: American
    Association for Higher Education, 1991.
The first part of Ewell's article provides a historical and political context for
assessment and sets the stage for part two—a critical review of current practice and includes extensive references.

Forrest, Aubrey, ed. *Time Will Tell: Portfolio-Assisted Assessment of General
    Education.* Washington: American Association for Higher Education,
    1990.
This report is a comprehensive guide to the implementation and use of student portfolios to assess general education outcomes at individual and program levels.

Hutchings, Pat. "Assessment and the Way We Work." Wiggins, Grant. "The
    Truth May Make You Free, but the Test May Keep You Imprisoned:
    Toward Assessment Worthy of the Liberal Arts." In *Assessment 1990:
    Understanding the Implications,* a volume of three presentations from the
    Fifth American Association for Higher Education Conference on
    Assessment in Higher Education, 1990.

Hutchings, Pat. *Behind Outcomes: Contexts and Questions for Assessment.*
    Washington: American Association for Higher Education, 1989.

Setting forth nine areas of inquiry for assessment that get "behind outcomes," Hutchings presents appropriate methods for addressing each area and resources for further work.

Hutchings, Pat, and Ted Marchese. "Watching Assessment: Questions, Stories, Prospects." *Change* 22 (September/October 1990).
Based on observations over a four-year period, Hutchings' and Marchese's article takes the reader to campuses for a first-hand look at assessment's effect.

Hutchings, Pat, Ted Marchese, and Barbara Wright. *Using Assessment to Strengthen General Education.* Washington: American Association for Higher Education, 1991.
This article is aimed at those familiar with assessment but not as familiar with recent developments in the field. It includes "Stories from the Field" (five campuses), resources, and reflections of assessment practitioners.

Involvement in Learning: Realizing the Potential of American Higher Education. Final Report of the Study Group on the Condition of Excellence in American Higher Education. Washington: National Institute of Education, 1985.

Paskow, Jacqueline, ed. *Assessment Programs and Projects: A Directory* (1987) Updated by Elizabeth A. Francis, (1990). Washington: American Association for Higher Education.
This report contains concise descriptions of thirty assessment projects implemented on campuses across the country.

Rossman, J. E., and Elaine El-Khawas. "Thinking About Assessment: Perspectives for Presidents and Chief Academic Officers." Washington: American Council on Education and American Association for Higher Education, 1987.
Aimed at administrators, this article provides an overview of assessment.

Shapiro, Joan Poliner. "Nonfeminist and Feminist Students at Risk: The Use of Case Study Analysis While Transforming the Postsecondary Curriculum." *Women's Studies International Forum* 13 (1990): 553–64.
This paper turns to the use of case studies of students to help create a more positive learning environment in women's studies classrooms. It is an at-

tempt to remove a chilly classroom climate from feminist classes by enabling students to understand and respect differences.

Shapiro, Joan P., Ann Butchart, and Cynthia Secor. "Illuminative Evaluation: Assessment of the Transportability of a Management Training Program for Women in Higher Education." *Educational Evaluation and Policy Analysis* 5 (1983): 456–71.
This is a very early description of the use of illuminative evaluation and its compatibility with women's studies projects. It shows how effective this form of evaluation can be with feminist projects because it combines qualitative and quantitative assessment and allows the problem to define the methods.

Shapiro, Joan P., and Beth Reed. "Considerations of Ethical Issues in the Assessment of Feminist Projects: A Case Study Using Illuminative Evaluation." In *Feminist Ethics and Social Science Research*, Nebraska Feminist Collective, eds. New York: Mellon Press, 1988.
This chapter focuses on ethics as it relates to evaluating feminist projects. Illuminative evaluation in relationship to feminist projects is explored, but the concept of objectivity in the assessment process is critiqued.

Shapiro, Joan P., and Beth Reed. "Illuminative Evaluation: Meeting the Special Needs of Feminist Projects." *Humanity and Society* 8 (1984): 432–41.
This article argues that illuminative evaluation is especially useful for feminist projects because it assumes that total objectivity in evaluation is neither possible nor desirable and because it is well-suited to innovative projects.

Shapiro, Joan P., and Carroll Smith-Rosenberg. "The 'Other Voices' in Contemporary Ethical Dilemmas: The Value of the New Scholarship on Women in the Teaching of Ethics." *Women's Studies International Forum* 12 (1989): 199–211.
This article demonstrates the use of students' journal entries to assess student learning. Through their own words, students show growth in understanding differences and analyses of complex ethical situations.

Stark, Joan S., Kathleen M. Shaw, and Malcolm A. Lowther. "Student Goals for College and Courses: A Missing Link in Assessing and Improving Academic Achievement." ASHE-ERIC Report No. 6. Washington: ERIC

Clearinghouse on Higher Education, George Washington University, 1989.

Tetreault, Mary Kay Thompson. "Feminist Phase Theory: An Experience-Derived Evaluation Model." In *Journal of Higher Education* 56 (July/August 1985): 363–84.
This article is an extension of Tetreault's work on feminist phase theory.

Tetreault, Mary Kay Thompson. "Integrating Content About Women and Gender into the Curriculum." In *Multicultural Education: Issues and Perspectives*, James A. Banks and Cherry A. McGee Banks, eds. Boston: Allyn and Beacon, 1989.
To create a gender-balanced multicultural curriculum where gender is interwoven with ethnicity, race, and class, Tetreault introduces the concept of feminist phase theory. She divides curricular thinking into five common phases: male-defined, contribution, bifocal, women's, and gender-balanced.

Wright, Barbara. "An Assessment Primer." *Metropolitan Universities: An International Forum* 3 (Spring 1993): 7–15.
Barbara Wright, former Director of the American Association for Higher Education's Assessment Forum, has written an introductory essay exploring the relation of assessment to improving teaching and learning. As guest editor for the Spring 1993 issue on assessment for *Metropolitan Universities*, Wright includes articles on portfolios, performance assessment in professional majors, assessment and diversity, and participatory assessment. See also several assessment articles in Volume 4, Number 1.

PERIODICAL
Assessment Update. Trudy W. Banta, ed. Knoxville, Tenn.: Center for Assessment Research and Development, University of Tennessee–Knoxville. Published quarterly by Jossey-Bass.
Begun in spring 1989, this publication's regular features include "Campus Profiles," which describes assessment projects at different campuses; "From The States," which reviews state-mandated assessment initiatives; information about projects at community colleges; recent developments in assessment; opinions; and new publications.